Agatha Raisin
COMPANION

Agatha Raisin
COMPANION

Introduction by
M.C. Beaton

CONSTABLE • LONDON

Constable & Robinson Ltd
3 The Lanchesters
162 Fulham Palace Road
London W6 9ER
www.constablerobinson.com

First published in the UK by Constable,
an imprint of Constable & Robinson, 2010

A copy of the British Library Cataloguing in Publication
Data is available from the British Library

UK ISBN: 978-1-84901-319-2

Printed and bound in the EU

1 3 5 7 9 10 8 6 4 2

Contents

Introduction

The writing road leading to Agatha Raisin is a long one.

When I left school, I became a fiction buyer for John Smith & Son Ltd in St Vincent Street, Glasgow, the oldest bookshop in Britain – alas, now closed. Those were the days when bookselling was a profession and one had to know something about every book in the shop.

I developed an eye for what sort of book a customer might want and could, for example, spot an arriving request for a leather-bound pocket-sized edition of Omar Khayyám at a hundred paces.

Mills & Boon romances were rather frowned on and were kept at the back of the fiction stand to be ready for ladies who asked me for 'a book with nothing, you know, *nasty* in it'.

As staff were allowed to borrow books, I was able to feed my addiction for detective and spy stories. As a child, my first love had been Richard Hannay in John Buchan's *The Thirty-Nine Steps*. Then, on my eleventh birthday, I was given a copy of Dorothy Sayers' *Lord Peter Views the Body* and read everything

by that author I could get. After that came, courtesy of the bookshop, Ngaio Marsh, Josephine Tey, Gladys Mitchell, Eric Ambler, Agatha Christie and very many more.

But I was desperate to write. I even offered my services free in Renfrew to a local paper, sure they would want me, as they appeared to have not very high standards, along with some terrible typos. I remember seeing, 'The Provost and his wife entered the gaily decorated hell.' I was particularly fond of the description of a wedding: 'The marriage of Miss Blank and Mr Bloggs was consummated at the altar to the sound of the organ.'

Having read Dorothy Sayers' *Murder Must Advertise*, I then decided to become a copywriter and sent my résumé to all the advertising agencies in Glasgow. I only got one interview, with the boss of some agency whose name I forget. He looked me over from my Harris tweed coat to my high heels and said, 'I was curious to see you and to give you a bit of advice. Never, my dear, say you edited the school magazine. Never say you've had nothing published. Lie. Say you've been published in *Punch*, the *Spectator* or anything you can think of. Come back in a couple of years and I'll think about it.'

A pretty young actress, Jill Lubbock, who was 'resting', came to work in the bookshop and often took me over to the Citizens Theatre where I met the actors. I was stage-struck. The actress moved on. A bookseller, who started work in the second-hand

department, seemed to me rather grand and I was anxious to impress her. I told her I often went backstage at the Citizens Theatre and went for coffee with the actors, and I offered to take her. I took her to a performance of *Henry IV Part Two*. We went backstage and met Fulton Mackay and John Grieve. 'Oh,' they said, 'union meeting tonight. We're not going for coffee.'

I was disappointed but I said to my new friend that we would go to the café next door anyway. We had only been there a few minutes when all the actors walked in, carefully avoiding looking at me. The hard fact was that, without my pretty actress friend, I was nobody. I writhed with humiliation as only a teenager can.

Bookselling was a very genteel job. We were not allowed to call each other by our first names. I was given half an hour in the morning to go out for coffee, an hour and a half for lunch, and half an hour in the afternoon for tea.

I was having coffee one morning, when I was joined by a customer, Mary Kavanagh, who recognized me. She said she was features editor of the Glasgow edition of the *Daily Mail* and wanted a reporter to cover a production of *Cinderella* at the Rutherglen Rep that evening, because the editor's nephew was acting as one of the Ugly Sisters, but all the reporters refused to go.

'I'll go,' I said eagerly.

She looked at me doubtfully. 'Have you had anything published?'

'Oh, yes,' I said, lying in my teeth. '*Punch, The Listener*, things like that.'

'Well, it's only fifty words,' she said doubtfully. 'All right.'

And that was the start. I rose up through vaudeville and then became lead theatre critic at the age of nineteen.

After that, I became fashion editor of *Scottish Field* magazine and then moved to the *Scottish Daily Express* as Scotland's new emergent writer and proceeded to submerge. The news editor gave me a try-out to save me from being sacked and I became a crime reporter.

People often ask if this experience was to help me in the future with writing detective stories. Yes, but not in the way they think. The crime in Glasgow was awful: razor gangs, axe men, reporting stories in filthy gaslit tenements where the stair lavatory had broken, and so, as an escape, I kept making up stories in my head which had nothing to do with reality. It all became too much for me and I got a transfer to the *Daily Express* in Fleet Street, London, where I found to my dismay that I was back in the fashion department, running around shows in hot salons, pinning up models' dresses in studios and feeling diminished.

It took me three months to get back to reporting. It was that terrible winter of 1963. I was living with a friend of my mother's in the Vale of Health on Hampstead Heath. There

were power cuts and gas cuts and then the water pipes in the road burst and I had to trudge up to the standpipe in Hampstead High Street to fetch water.

Women on the newspaper were not allowed to wear boots or trousers, and high heels were a must. Flat heels could get you sent home. I can vividly remember the awful cold of that winter. Come late spring and I was called into the newsroom and told to visit the home of John Profumo, the Secretary of State for War, get his wife aside, and ask her what she thought of her husband shacking up with a cabinet whore. I had a sinking feeling I had got the job because I was considered expendable.

When the polite butler told me that they were out visiting the constituency, I could have kissed him, I felt so relieved. I subsequently met Christine Keeler and Mandy Rice-Davies. Christine Keeler photographed like a dream but was not so attractive in real life whereas Mandy was pretty. If you remember, the scandal was that Christine was also sleeping with the Russian military attaché at the same time as John Profumo.

A lot of my reporting on this story consisted of doorstepping Stephen Ward, the man who was accused of pimping the two girls.

Then one day, I was sent to interview Sir Oswald Mosley at his headquarters in Victoria and then follow him on his march down the Strand. I was a child of the Second World War and was appalled at the brown shirts and Nazi armbands worn by his

supporters. Still, a job was a job and I walked with him down the Strand. To my horror, footage of the march appeared on BBC news that evening, the presenter saying, 'Oswald Mosley and some of his faithful followers,' and there I was, right at the front. I couldn't help wondering what former schoolteachers and friends would think when they saw me.

For a while, as I was six characters in search of an author, I enjoyed being a Fleet Street reporter. I would walk down Fleet Street in the evening if I was on the late shift and feel the thud of the printing presses and smell the aroma of hot paper and see St Paul's, floodlit, floating above Ludgate Hill, and felt I had truly arrived.

I became chief woman reporter just as boredom and reality were setting in. That was when I met my husband, Harry Scott Gibbons, former Middle East correspondent for the paper who had just resigned to write a book, *The Conspirators*, about the British withdrawal from Aden.

I resigned as well and we went on our travels, through Greece, Turkey and Cyprus. Harry was now engaged on writing a book about the Cyprus troubles. We arrived back in London, broke, and I had a baby, Charles. We moved to America when Harry found work as an editor on the *Oyster Bay Guardian*, a Long Island newspaper. That was not a very pleasant experience.

After various adventures, down and out in Virginia, we got jobs on Rupert Murdoch's new tabloid, the *National Star*, now

The Star, Harry as deputy news editor and me on the picture desk. Harry then got a job on another tabloid in Greenwich, Connecticut, which meant I could stay at home and look after Charles, who was now attending a school for gifted children in Brooklyn Heights. We were living in a Mafia-controlled area, the Gallo boys reigned supreme, and my son was driven to school by Nicky the Kid.

But I longed to write. I had read all Georgette Heyer's Regency romances and thought I would try some of the new ones that were coming out. I complained to my husband, 'They're awful. The history's wrong, the speech is wrong and the dress is wrong.'

'Well, write one,' he urged.

My mother had been a great fan of the Regency period and I had been brought up on Jane Austen and various history books. She even found out-of-print books of the period such as Maria Edgeworth's *Moral Tales*. I remember with affection a villain called Lord Raspberry. So I cranked up the film in my head and began to write what was there. The first book was called *Regency Gold*. I had only done about twenty pages, blocked by the thought that surely I couldn't really write a whole book, when my husband took them from me and showed them to a writer friend who recommended an agent. So I

went on and wrote the first fifty pages and plot and sent it all to the agent, Barbara Lowenstein. She suggested some changes, and after making them I took the lot back to her.

The book sold in three days flat. Then, before it was even finished, I got an offer from another publisher to write Edwardian romances, which I did under the name of Jennie Tremaine because my maiden name, Marion Chesney, was contracted to the first publisher. Other publishers followed, other names: Ann Fairfax, Helen Crampton and Charlotte Ward.

I was finally contracted by St Martin's Press to write six hardback Regency series at a time.

I had written over a hundred historical novels when we visited Sutherland in the north of Scotland for a holiday. We joined a fishing school in Lochinver to learn to fly cast for salmon. But while the others were trying to catch something – anything – I dreamt of writing a detective story. The setting was marvellous: eleven people out in the magnificent wilds of Sutherland. I swear I could practically see a dead body rolling down the salmon pools.

When I got back to New York, I discussed my ambition with my editor at St Martin's Press, Hope Dellon. 'Okay,' she said, 'Who's your detective?' I had only got as far as the rough idea and hadn't thought of one. 'The village bobby,' I said hurriedly. 'What's his name?' I quickly racked my brains. 'Hamish Macbeth.'

I had to find not only a name for my detective but a new name

for myself. 'Give me a name that isn't Mac something,' suggested Hope.

So I quoted from the Border Ballads: 'Yestreen the Queen had four Maries/The night she'll hae but three/There was Marie Seaton and Marie Beaton/And Marie Carmichael and me.'

Hope said that M.C. Beaton would be a good name, keeping the M.C. for Marion Chesney.

So I began to write detective stories. We moved back to London to further our son's education and it was there that the idea for the first Agatha Raisin was germinated, but I did not know it at the time.

My son's housemaster asked me if I could produce some of my excellent home baking for a charity sale. I did not want to let my son down by telling him I couldn't bake. So I went to Waitrose and bought two quiches, carefully removed the shop wrappings, put my own wrappings on with a homemade label, and delivered them. They were a great success.

Shortly afterwards, Hope Dellon, who is very fond of the Cotswolds, asked me if I would consider writing a detective story set in that scenic area. I wanted the detective to be a woman. I had enjoyed E.F. Benson's Miss Mapp books and thought it might be interesting to create a detective that the reader might not like but nonetheless would want to win in the end. I was also inspired by the amusing detective stories of Colin Watson in his Flaxborough novels and Simon Brett's detective, Charles Paris.

We had moved to the Cotswolds by that point, and I gave Agatha Raisin my own experiences of being buried alive in winter. Then I remembered cheating with the quiche. What if Agatha did the same thing for a quiche-baking competition, and the judge dropped dead of poisoning? She would be exposed as a fraud and would need to solve the case to save face. And so the first book, *The Quiche of Death*, was born.

I had never had any literary ambitions as a writer. I only wanted to produce something that would entertain on, say, a wet day or when someone wanted an escape. When I worked in the book trade, no one talked about literary writers, but there were magnificent storytellers then: Neville Shute, Rose Macaulay, Agatha Christie, J.R.R. Tolkien, Hammond Innes, Ian Fleming and so many more.

I had noticed in New York that people were reading a lot of old detective stories because there seemed to be nothing to read between the Mills & Boon romances and the Booker Prize novels. I was lucky to get published at the beginning of the boom, because now there are all sorts of detectives, from cats to rabbis.

I also find that political correctness in this nanny state has gone a bit too far. Although I don't use real people in my books, I do borrow some real incidents for the rebellious Agatha. In Sutherland, a printer friend, before the smoking ban, was out in a restaurant for dinner with his wife. Seeing a large glass ashtray on the table, they lit up. A man and woman at the next table

pointedly began coughing and flapping their hands. The printer called over the maître d' and said, 'Find these people another table. They're annoying us.'

Agatha drinks black coffee, smokes, wears fur coats and can't cook. Her idea of dinner is to nuke a curry in the microwave.

I wanted a character who is good to be an antidote to my abrasive Agatha and so I invented Mrs Bloxby, the vicar's wife. It is quite difficult to write about good people: easy to write about bad ones. But really good people fascinate me, and in these wicked days there are more of them around than you would think.

Agatha is rather emotionally retarded and so is an obsessive romantic where men are concerned. Along comes James Lacey, a retired colonel, and Agatha falls head over heels, simply because subconsciously she knows he is unobtainable. He maintains a rather cold distance, even after they are briefly married.

Young policeman Bill Wong is Agatha's first friend, one who sees the soft centre under the truculent exterior.

None of the characters grow any older. If you age your detective, sooner or later you have to pension him or her off. Agatha has a perpetual battle with the ravages of middle age and manages to maintain a good appearance.

Her rather camp friend, Roy Silver, moves in and out of her life, as does Sir Charles Fraith, a character with whom she has a brief fling although she never really knows what he thinks of her.

I am often asked if I write with a specific audience in mind and the answer to that is, no. I write as near as I can to the books I enjoy most. Writers who try to copy someone else's success always come a cropper. It's known as 'bandwagonning'. I was asked recently by a publisher if I would consider a series of detective stories set in Paris. I knew this was because of the success of *The Da Vinci Code* so I refused, saying I didn't understand the French.

On one occasion, a woman said to me with a sigh, 'Well, I might prostitute myself one day and write one of those little Mills & Boon romances.' Of course, Agatha would have said, 'Lady, you couldn't even prostitute yourself,' but I am much too polite. Successful romance writers are writing as well as they can. It's no use writing down. I, for example, lack the necessary skill to write a modern romance.

Agatha Raisin will continue to live in the Cotswolds because the very placid beauty of the place, with its winding lanes and old

cottages, serves as a contrast to the often abrasive Agatha. I am only sorry that I continue to inflict so much murder and mayhem on this tranquil setting.

Hope Dellon is still my editor for the Agatha Raisin books at St Martin's Press, Krystyna Green is my editor at Constable & Robinson in London, and the charismatic Barbara Lowenstein is still my agent.

Will Agatha and James Lacey ever get together again? I don't know.

But if they do, you'll be the first to know.

M.C. Beaton

1
Introducing Agatha

We first meet the formidable Mrs Raisin at the newly cleared desk of her public relations firm, Raisin Promotions, in the smart surrounds of Mayfair's South Molton Street. She is fifty-three, and about to launch into a long-dreamed-of retirement in the Cotswolds after a hugely successful career which has made her very wealthy. She is 'a stocky, middle-aged woman with a round, pugnacious face and small, bearlike eyes. Her hair, brown and healthy, is cut in a short, square style, established in the heyday of Mary Quant and not much changed since. Her legs were good and her clothes expensive.'

Although a life in the tranquil valleys of the Cotswolds is one she has always dreamed of, it is not long before Agatha is lonely and bored. The guarded politeness of the villagers leads her to believe she will never fit in and she misses the hustle and bustle of London. She soon realizes that her work had also been her social life and that she has no true friends. Her first foray into village life, passing off a shop-bought quiche as her own in a local competition, ends in disaster

when the judge is poisoned. Ironically, it is that very act, and her subsequent solving of the crime, that sees Agatha truly accepted by her neighbours.

Character

Agatha is a strong-willed, strident lady who never suffers fools gladly. She can be hugely insensitive, even to her closest friends, and tends to bulldoze her way through life not understanding that her manner and comments alienate people. Underneath her tough exterior, she is a mass of insecurities and frequently feels vulnerable, especially about her upbringing, her age and her looks. She is prone to falling in love and is hopelessly romantic, dreaming of Hollywood happy endings and scripting them in her head whenever her heart is aroused.

Smoking

Imploring Agatha to give up smoking only brings out her stubborn streak.

'When would people grasp the simple fact that if you wanted people to stop smoking, then don't nag them and make them feel guilty… smokers were hounded and berated, causing all the rebellion of the hardened addict.' (*Love from Hell*)

Agatha gives up smoking after meeting Jimmy Jessop in *Witch of Wyckhadden* and becoming

friends with the elderly residents of the Garden Hotel. She lasts a few days, but gives in to her craving after the body of the second victim is found floating in the sea.

Comments from her new neighbour, John Armitage, who tells her that 'smoking is a sure way to ruin your eyesight and give you lots of lines around the mouth', prompt her to kick the habit again. In *Day the Floods Came*, she visits a hypnotist in Gloucester who makes her think that every cigarette tastes 'terrible, like burning rubber' as soon as it is lit. This new resolve lasts until the beginning of the next case, *Curious Curate*, when the hypnotic spell wears off.

The long-threatened government smoking ban finally arrives in *Spoonful of Poison*, to the horror of dedicated nicotine addict Agatha. When she lights up in the village pub, landlord John Fletcher immediately takes her cigarette away from her. 'Stalinist bureaucrats,' mutters a disgruntled Agatha. Now forced to smoke

outside, she throws her weight behind the purchase of a smoking shelter for the pub.

Superstition

Despite her no-nonsense approach to most aspects of life, Agatha is occasionally taken in by the superstitious and supernatural. In *Fairies of Fryfam*, for example, she consults a fortune teller who informs her that her destiny lies in Norfolk. Lonely and fed up, she believes every word and puts her house up for sale, renting a cottage in the county with a view to moving there.

Jealousy

Although she refuses to admit it to herself, Agatha is prone to stabs of envy in both her love life and her professional life. She is a huge lover of the limelight and hates to have anyone else taking the credit for the case, especially if that someone is younger and prettier.

In *There Goes the Bride*, her jealousy of Toni, who manages to solve a high-profile missing teenager case and make the national papers, prompts her to give her young colleague all the small cases at the agency. When Toni confronts her, she is disarmingly honest and admits it: 'Even if I'd broken the case, the photographers and reporters have only got to see you and they forget I exist,' she sighs. In the past, she has been magnanimous to her fellow snoops, such as Roy and Phil, but has always bitterly regretted it when it is their story that appears in the paper.

When it comes to love, her jealousy can take a more extreme form, particularly when it concerns James. On finding her husband drinking with Melissa Sheppard, for instance, she accuses the attractive divorcée of being a 'trollop', then calls James a 'philandering bastard' and threatens to kill him before pouring a tankard of beer over his head.

Religion

Agatha has no religious leaning, although she often attends church in order to keep in with the villagers and to please her great friend, Mrs Bloxby.

She has also been known to pray to 'Mrs Bloxby's God' in times of trouble. For example, when faced with a gun-wielding killer in *Love, Lies and Liquor*, 'She didn't know if there was a God, but Mrs Bloxby believed in one, so she asked Mrs Bloxby's God either to let her die with dignity or to save her.' The fact that her prayers are answered is never enough to convince her that the deity truly exists.

AGATHA'S FAVOURITE . . .

Exclamation: 'Snakes and bastards'

Perfume: Yves Saint Laurent Champagne

Breakfast: Four cigarettes and three strong cups of black coffee

Dessert: Toffee Pudding

Beauty Parlour: The Beaumonde Beauty Salon in Evesham where a 'pretty woman named Dawn' works wonders.

Ageing Disgracefully

Agatha hates the reality of getting older and when she develops arthritis in her hip, she chooses to ignore it, putting the nagging pain down to a pulled muscle. Anxious to avoid a hip operation, she even goes to a private doctor for a cortisone injection which costs her £1,000. But her wonderful masseur Richard frequently tells her she will soon need a hip replacement.

The problem begins in *Deadly Dance* when she becomes aware of a nagging pain. 'But her mind shrieked against the very idea of her having rheumatism or arthritis. Those were aliments of the elderly, surely.'

The realities of the middle-aged body are a depressing thought for Agatha, who does her utmost to hold the ravages of time at bay. After meeting new neighbour Paul Chatterton at the church, in *Haunted House*, Agatha pulls down her jumper to hide her stomach and vows to diet and exercise more. 'What a bore ageing was! Things drooped and sagged and bulged unless one worked ferociously on them.

The flesh under the chin was really showing a slackness which alarmed her. She had slapped herself under the chin sixty times that morning and had performed several grimacing exercises in order to try and tighten the flesh up.'

When faced with the effortless beauty of youth, in the shape of her assistant Toni or an attractive girl she meets on a case, Agatha's age leaves her feeling miserable.

'I feel on the outside looking in,' mourns Agatha in *Spoonful of Poison*, after being told the music playing in a hairdresser's is for young people. 'I feel trapped in an age group that's out of touch with every other age group.'

Fashion and Beauty

Agatha abhors cheap, badly made clothing and always dresses expensively. After a lifetime in power suits she only shops at the best boutiques and still favours wool two-pieces, expensive silk dresses and, when dressing down, well-cut linen trousers. Her heels are as high as she can get away with and she often finds herself unsuitably dressed for the job, preferring to show off her legs to their best advantage rather than opt for comfort.

Her outfits are chosen carefully, particularly for a date, when she will spend hours trying on every dress in the wardrobe. Her wedding day, in *Murderous Marriage*, is another chance to buy an expensive outfit to impress her man.

'She had picked out a white wool suit to be wed in. With it she

would wear a shady hat of straw with a wide brim, a green silk blouse, high-heeled black shoes and a spray of flowers on her lapel instead of a bouquet. At times, she did wish she were younger again so she could get married in white.'

Agatha spends a great deal of time and money on her appearance and is rarely seen without make-up. Her main wish is to turn back the hands of time, using top anti-wrinkle creams and beauty treatments, and she is quite demoralized by the slightest hint of ageing.

A grey hair or a sprouting growth on her lip can send shudders of horror through the normally immaculate detective and sends her screaming to the beauty parlour.

'She tried on the white suit again and then peered closely in the mirror at her face. Her bearlike eyes were too small but could be made to look larger on the great day with a little judicious application of mascara and eyeshadow. There were those nasty little wrinkles around her mouth and, to her horror, she saw a long hair sprouting from her upper lip and seized the tweezers and wrenched it out. She took off the precious suit, put on a blouse and trousers, and vigorously slapped anti-wrinkle cream all over her face.'

When Agatha feels terribly low, she occasionally lets her appearance slip, which is tantamount to a cry for help from the normally immaculate detective and one her friends pick up on very quickly. In *Perfect Paragon*, for example, Charles notices that

her waistline is expanding and she has forgotten to apply make-up. 'He couldn't remember Agatha ever forgetting to put on make-up before.' Bill Wong is also worried about her lack of grooming, prompting her into action. Seeing herself in the mirror she realizes 'her hair was limp, her skin was shiny and she had a spot on her nose. Worse, she could see the shadow of an incipient moustache on her upper lip.' A quick trip to Evesham, for a facial, a seaweed wrap and a visit to the hairdresser's, has our heroine back on track.

Occasionally Agatha dabbles with a radical change in looks, usually finding herself dissatisfied with the results. In *Curious Curate*, she wonders if blondes really do have more fun and decides to find out. After the hairdresser has dyed her hair a 'warm honey-blonde' she entertains Bill and his new girlfriend, who instantly becomes jealous of their relationship. Although this amuses her young friend, Agatha begins to feel her new look is too brassy and resolves to go back to her natural brown colouring.

Battling the Bulge

London life, and walking everywhere to beat the traffic, had kept Agatha trim despite the expensive dinners that were an everyday part of the job. Country life means that she is soon driving everywhere in the car and this, combined with a love of comfort food and microwave meals, and a distinct lack of willpower, means she is soon putting on weight.

Soon after moving to the country, she discovers that she can't fasten her skirt and has put on an inch and a half around the waist. 'Carsely was not going to make Agatha Raisin let herself go!' she vows, and she buys a bicycle to help her exercise. This is the start of a constant battle with the bulge which sends her from pub lunches with sticky toffee pudding to Pilates classes, a brief spell in a ramblers' association and various other short-lived diet and exercise plans.

THE RAISIN DIET

(Not recommended by nutritionists)

Breakfast

Strong black coffee (three cups)
Cigarettes

Lunch

Steak and kidney pudding with chips
Or　Pub lasagne and chips
Or　All day breakfast – egg, bacon,
sausage and beans
Followed by toffee pudding

Dinner

Extra-hot microwaved
vindaloo
Or Microwaved lasagne

Snacks

Mrs Bloxby's teacakes

Drinks

Gin and Tonic
White wine
Coffee
Tea

2
Agatha's Past

Agatha's unhappy childhood in the
Birmingham slums often comes back
to haunt her, although she is proud of
her achievements since. She was born in a tower
block, the only daughter of Joseph and Margaret Styles,
both unemployed alcoholics. Home life was terrible and
even if they managed to scrape enough together to take their
daughter on holiday, there was no joy in it for her. When
Charles asks her where she went on holiday as a child,
'Agatha remembered occasional holidays at holiday camps
with a shudder. Her parents were usually drunk and raucous.'
Her only journey abroad as a child was a day trip to France.

As a poverty-stricken child, Agatha dreamed of receiving
her first pay packet and walking into a sweet shop to buy all
the chocolate she wanted. 'But by the time that happened,
her desires focused on a pair of purple high-heeled shoes
with bows.'

Agatha was bright at school but very shy and sensitive.
Life's hard knocks taught her to develop a shell and she

feigned an aggressive nature to keep other pupils away. At fifteen, her parents thought she was old enough to earn some money and made her leave school for a dull job in a biscuit factory. She disliked the women she worked with but hated being at home even more, so, in order to get out as fast as she could, she worked overtime and saved as much money as she could.

Disgusted by her parents' behaviour, she finally took her savings and bolted to London, leaving without saying goodbye when they were both in a drunken stupor. Settling in the big city, she waited tables seven days a week at a restaurant she later described as 'a bit like one of those Lyon's Corner Houses. Good food but not French'. She used her tips to pay for shorthand and typing lessons, and secured a good position as a secretary in a public relations firm. There she set about learning the trade, but her studies were interrupted by a brief and disastrous relationship with Jimmy Raisin, who she foolishly married.

Once away from her violent drunk of a husband, she threw herself into work and became a rising star in PR, choosing expensive clothes and getting the results she wanted from journalists and clients with a mixture of cajoling, bullying and blackmail.

Her ambition and ruthlessness eventually led to her starting her own PR firm, Raisin Promotions, and being the boss suited her down to the ground. She had a smart office in South Molton Street, a flat in Mayfair, and a new accent to match. The financial

rewards were substantial and Agatha became a very rich woman. All the hard work, however, had been a means to an end. As a child, when she was taken on a rare holiday by her parents, she had dreamed of a cottage in the Cotswolds. 'Her parents had hated it, and had said that they should have gone to the Butlin's Holiday Camp as usual, but to Agatha the Cotswolds represented everything she wanted in life; beauty, tranquillity and security. So even as a child, she had become determined that one day she would live in one of those pretty cottages in a quiet, peaceful village, far from the noise and smells of the city.'

At fifty-three, Agatha finally decided to realize her dream, so she sold her business and found her dream cottage in the village of Carsely. While the cottage was perfect, and the village of Carsely friendly, Agatha soon missed the hustle and bustle of London and often felt lonely in her new home. That was, until she found her new calling as an amateur sleuth.

Agatha has put her childhood and her parents, who are now dead, firmly behind her and her accent belies her true upbringing. Occasionally, however, in times of extreme stress, her Birmingham twang creeps in and her impoverished background often leaves her with a feeling of inferiority when she is mixing in the upper echelons of society. When she first meets Sir Charles, for instance, 'she found she was dithering over the idea of having lunch with a baronet. Logic screamed at her that Sir

Charles was a mere baronet who lived in a Victorian mansion described in the guidebooks as "architecturally undistinguished". Deep down, the old Agatha, product of the Birmingham slum, trembled.'

In *Day the Floods Came*, Agatha assumes John Armitage only made his ungallant pass at her because she revealed her true background to him. After she'd told him his detective story, set in the Birmingham slums, didn't ring true, he asked how she knew. 'I told him because we'd had a fair bit to drink. He propositioned me, just like that. He hadn't uttered one word of praise about my appearance. He hadn't shown me any affection, he hadn't even shown me he desired me. So I thought it was because of my poor background he felt he could dispense with the preliminaries,' she tells a friend later.

Even so, Agatha's driving ambition is the one thing that has prevented her from wallowing in the past. 'Ambition is a great drug,' she says. 'I just forged ahead the whole time. Never really looked back at yesterday.'

Jimmy Raisin

While she was still very young and new to London, Agatha fell in love with Jimmy. One night, he came into the restaurant where she was working as a waitress, with 'a rather tarty blonde, a bit older than him'. The couple seemed to be at odds and he amused himself by flirting with Agatha. That evening, as she left work, he

was waiting for her and asked to walk her home. She liked his light-hearted, jovial banter and the pair got on well. However, when they reached her tiny bedsit in Kilburn, Jimmy confessed he was homeless and Agatha said he could sleep on the couch, for one night only. The next day, they had a day out at the zoo, which was not to Agatha's taste but, as she later told James, 'I had been so very lonely and here I was with a handsome fellow of my own and it all seemed marvellous.'

Somehow, Jimmy ended up moving into the flat and, as Agatha was not keen on getting pregnant out of wedlock, Jimmy laughed and suggested they got married. They tied the knot in London and had a brief honeymoon in Blackpool. Jimmy, she later revealed, 'was the only man in my life who ever made me feel pretty'. Before the relationship went sour, 'He made me feel good, made me feel exhilarated, as if the world was a funny place where nothing much mattered.'

After a month, during which Jimmy found a job loading newspapers, Agatha realized that she had merely switched a drunken home life with her parents for an alcoholic husband. The

drunkenness soon bred violence, although the feisty Agatha hit back because she was 'still thin but pretty wiry'. After losing his job, Jimmy drifted in and out of work and drank more and more. After each bout of drinking, he would be contrite and promise to turn their lives around, and Agatha stood by him for two years. By then she had landed a good job in a PR firm and decided to spend her cash on a decent wardrobe rather than keeping Jimmy in drink.

One evening, Agatha came home from work and found Jimmy in a drunken stupor. She opened the post, found some leaflets from Alcoholics Anonymous that she had sent off for, and made a life-changing decision. She pinned the literature to his chest, packed her bag and walked out.

Although he knew where she worked, Jimmy never came looking for his missing wife and stayed away for many a year. Agatha was convinced he was dead until the day he turned up to ruin her marriage to James, and ended up a murder victim.

3
Agatha's Cotswolds

Carsely

The nearest station is Moreton-in-Marsh. From there Agatha drives up through Bourton-on-the-Hill on the A44, then turns off the main road to drive into the fictional village of Carsely.

Moreton is situated on the other side of the Fosse Way (A44) from Blockley, ten miles from Evesham and six miles from Moreton-in-Marsh.

Mircester

Agatha's nearest, fictional, town and the site of the frequently visited police station where her friend Bill Wong is based. An old town with cobbled streets which is dominated by a great medieval abbey, it boasts a few restaurants, pubs and a nightlife which includes the Happy Night Club, in a dingy back street. It was here that murder victim Jessica Bradley enjoyed her last night out before she was found dead in a ditch off the dual carriageway outside the town.

Agatha finds offices in the town when she sets up her agency in *Deadly Dance*.

Ancombe

The fictional village of Ancombe is Carsely's closest neighbour and is two miles from Carsely. 'Ancombe was one of those Cotswold villages about the size of Broad Campden that seemed too perfect to be true. Very small, but with an old church in the centre, thatched cottages, beautiful gardens and everything with a manicured air.' (*Murderous Marriage*)

The Carsely Ladies' Society often socializes with the Ancombe Ladies' Society and attends their amateur shows and events. Mabel Smedley, the wife of victim Robert in *Perfect Paragon*, is a member who lives in the village.

Ancombe has a village shop and a church, but little else. The local pub, The Feathers, serves very good food, but is very pricey. Agatha first encounters it in *Quiche of Death* when the Cummings-Brownes join her for dinner there and she foots the bill.

It is also the site of the eighteenth-century ancient spring, fashioned in the shape of a skull, which leads to two murders in *Wellspring of Death*. A Miss Jakes had discovered the water source in her garden and had it channelled through a pipe in her wall and into a fountain, to be used by the 'weary traveller'. It is still thought to have restorative properties and is well used by

passing walkers. After the Ladies' Society gets heated about a water company's plans to use the spring there, and Agatha is offered the PR job by the same company, she walks to the village and finds a dead body.

Dembley

A fictional market town in Gloucestershire, which provided the setting for the fourth Raisin book, *Walkers of Dembley*. Agatha and James, posing as a married couple, borrow a flat in Sheep Street belonging to Sir Charles Fraith. The walkers favour a pub called The Grapes, but there is another one called The Fleece. Terry and Peter, both members of the ramblers' group, work at a restaurant called The Copper Kettle. There is also a primary school where victims Jessica and Jeffrey worked with suspect Deborah.

Blockley

Blockley is the actual home of author M.C. Beaton. The picturesque village is 'a few miles from Carsely', across the A44 and then down a hill, and lies between Moreton-in-Marsh and Evesham. The once-thriving mills have been turned into homes and the property prices are sky high. 'The village is dominated by a square-towered church, and by Georgian terraces of mellow Cotswold stone. The long, straggling main street used to be full of little shops, but only the many-paned shop windows, lovingly

preserved, remain to show where they once stood.' (*Love from Hell*)

Although an exceptionally pretty village, it remains off the tourist drag and receives little of the attention that Stow-on-the-Wold and Bourton-on-the-Water attract. There is a post-office-cum-general store, which Agatha and Charles visit to find the whereabouts of the ex-husband of murder victim Melissa Sheppard in *Love from Hell*. Charles bemoans the fact that the road into the attractive village is ruined by trucks going to a nearby industrial estate.

Moreton-in-Marsh

A beautiful market town with the tree-lined Fosse Way, an old Roman military road, running through it. 'Ever since the Abbot of Westminster, who owned the land, decided to make use of the transport on the Fosse Way and a new Moreton was built in 1222, it has been a favourite shopping place for travellers, the wool merchants of medieval times being replaced with tourists.'

King Charles I granted a charter for the market in 1638 and later stayed at the large pub, The White Hart, in the centre of the town.

Moreton-in-Marsh was used as a coaching station before the coming of the Oxford to Worcester railway in 1853 and now has a mainline train station, connecting to Paddington, which is the nearest to Carsely. Hence it was the gateway to the Cotswolds

when Agatha first arrived, as well as the station Roy usually arrives at. Agatha enjoys shopping at the Tuesday market and has the occasional lamb stew in The White Hart.

Ashton-Le-Walls

Ten miles outside Mircester, this small, fictional village is the site of the health farm, Hunters Field, where Jimmy Raisin stayed before wrecking Agatha's wedding to James in *Murderous Marriage.*

Hebberden

A tiny, fictional village on the other side of Ancombe from Carsely. Nestling in a valley, the picturesque huddle of cottages is served by one pub and no shops. Agatha and Paul Chatterton investigate a reported haunting at Ivy Cottage, a large thatched cottage in the village before the owner, a Mrs Witherspoon, dies.

Stow-on-the-Wold

A historic market town of mellow Cotswold stone, set high on a hill in Gloucestershire, four miles from Moreton-in-Marsh. Most of the houses date back to the sixteenth century and it boasts one of the oldest pubs in England, the Royalist Inn, which incorporates the original building of the Eagle and Child, dating from the year 947.

The town is very touristy and its tiny central parking area is the scene of many a small victory over the visitors for Agatha. Her beloved masseur, Richard Rasdall, practises above the sweet shop, The Honey Pot, which is run by his 'pretty wife', Lyn. Richard and Lyn are real people and The Honey Pot is a real sweet shop in Church Street.

Evesham

'Cynics say Evesham is famous for dole and asparagus.' The River Avon runs through the town, famous for its fruit and vegetable trade, which nestles in the Vale of Evesham and boasts many ancient churches and historical buildings. But it also has a sadder air and can present itself as a 'down-at-heel town. Despite the increasing population, shops keep closing up and the boards over the windows are decorated with old Evesham scenes by local artists, so that sometimes it seems a town of pictures and thrift shops.' Agatha observes that the

town seems to be full of 'enormous, fecund women' with pushchairs and leggings.

In *Wizard of Evesham*, Agatha and Charles visit the Almonry, a rambling fourteenth-century building which now houses the museum. Hairdresser Mr John runs a salon in the high street and lives in a villa in Cheltenham Road, where Agatha is almost burned to death after his murder.

Kylie Stokes is found, by Agatha, floating in the swollen river there in *Day the Floods Came*. Her boyfriend runs the Hollywood Nights club in the town with his father. Harrison Peterson is also killed while staying in the town in *Deadly Dance*.

Herris Cum Magna

A tiny, fictional village off the Stow–Burford road, where the Laggatt-Browns live in the manor house in *Deadly Dance*. 'The manor house itself was one of those low, rambling Cotswold stone buildings that are much larger inside than they seem from the outside.'

Comfrey Magna

'An odd, secretive-looking fictional village,' built along a drove road near Carsely. All the houses are old and on the one thoroughfare, and most of the inhabitants are almost as ancient as their homes. A Norman church, which Cromwell's followers robbed of its stained-glass windows, and a large, grey vicarage dominate the village, which also has one small pub, called The Grunty Man. In *Spoonful of Poison*, Agatha helps the vicar by getting an A-list star to open the fête, but the jam-tasting leads to chaos when the preserves are laced with a hallucinogenic drug.

4
Carsely

Carsely is a beautiful village which 'nestles in a fold of the Cotswold hills' just off the A44. The route into the village passes through a tunnel of trees which always signal homecoming to Agatha when she returns from her travels.

Built around a Cotswold-stone high street, it consists of two long lines of houses, interspersed with shops, 'some low and thatched, some warm gold brick with slate roofs'. The village post-office-cum-general store, where Agatha buys most of her microwave meals and cat food, is called Harveys. The other shops include an old-fashioned haberdasher's, a butcher's and 'a shop that seemed to sell nothing other than dried flowers and to be hardly ever open'. The pretty cottages 'leaned together as if for support in their old age. The gardens were bright with cherry blossom, forsythia and daffodils.'

The warm, traditional pub, the Red Lion, stands at one end of the high street and the church and vicarage, home to Mr and Mrs Bloxby, at the other end. A few tiny streets

ramble off the main drag, providing space for the odd cottage or two.

Outside the village, and barely visible from the high street, is a council estate. A police station, a primary school and a library are placed in between the two.

Agatha's Cottage

Agatha's home is a thatched, detached cottage of golden Cotswold stone at the end of Lilac Lane, just off the high street. 'It looked like a cottage in one of those calendars she used to treasure as a girl.' Low, recently rethatched with Norfolk reed, with a small garden at the front and a long, narrow one at the back, it is separated from the only other cottage in the lane by a narrow path. Although it had no official name, it was originally known to the locals as Budgen's Cottage, after a villager who had lived there some fifteen years before. Agatha soon makes it her own and has a sign made declaring its new name, Raisin's Cottage.

The house consists of a small hall, a dining room, a living room and a large, square kitchen, where Agatha spends most of her time. Upstairs are two beam-ceilinged bedrooms and a bathroom. Agatha had the entire house decorated by an interior designer but quickly scrapped the fake horse brasses and other twee country clichés after moving in. From the kitchen she enjoys a view of the Cotswold hills.

James Lacey's Cottage

The cottage next door, the only other dwelling in Lilac Lane, is separated from Agatha's cottage by a hedge and a narrow path. There is a small front garden and a back garden similar in size to Agatha's. The cottages are almost the same, except that Agatha's is thatched and the neighbouring home is tiled.

Church

The Church of St Jude, at one end of the high street, is a small, fourteenth-century building with stained-glass windows and long, wooden pews. Vicar Alf Bloxby presides over traditional Anglican services here and in two other local churches, meaning the Sunday communion in Carsely is unusually early, at 8.30 a.m.

Vicarage

An old house next to the church which has sloping floors, laid with floorboards 'polished like black glass'. The living room, where Mrs Bloxby entertains Agatha when it is too cold to sit in the garden, has an open wood fire, a large Persian rug and worn

feather-cushioned chairs. The scent of lavender and woodsmoke hangs in the air and there is 'an air of comfort and goodness about the place'. To the oft-troubled Agatha, the building is a welcome port in a storm.

Pub

The Red Lion is at the opposite end of the high street from the church. 'A jolly, low-raftered, chintzy sort of place', it is run by John (originally Joe) Fletcher who is an amiable landlord, although he is loath to come to Agatha's aid when she is abandoned by James and left homeless in *Murderous Marriage*, claiming there is no room at the inn.

On arrival in the village, Agatha finds the regulars chat to her with the 'sort of open friendliness that never went any further', which made her feel like an outsider.

Plumtrees Cottage

The home of Major Cummings-Browne and his wife and the scene of the first crime. On the main street of Carsely, opposite the church in a row of four, the ancient stone cottage fronts on to a cobbled, diamond-shaped area.

Rose Cottage

Phil Witherspoon's home is next to the primary school and, despite its old-fashioned name, is a modern building devoid of

roses. It is built from red brick, with a tarmac-covered front garden, so that he can park his car off the main street. Phil keeps it impeccably tidy and, despite the appearance of the front, spends a lot of time on his back garden, which he enjoys.

Other Houses

Murder victim Mrs Josephs lived in an 'undistinguished terrace of Victorian cottages at the top of the village' and Mary Fortune, also destined to become a victim, bought the same house.

5

A Pastime in Fighting Crime

Like all good amateur sleuths, trouble seems to follow Agatha around. Even if she escapes the murder-ridden hills of the Cotswolds, a mystery is sure to be lurking at her new destination.

Here, for the seasoned reader, is a recap of Mrs Raisin's adventures to date but, be warned, there may be one or two spoilers if you haven't yet read them all.

BOOK 1:
Agatha Raisin and the Quiche of Death

Retiring from a successful career in PR, Agatha has achieved a childhood dream and bought a cottage in the Cotswolds. But moving into the pretty village of Carsely is not the easy transition she assumes. She misses London, feels a

real sense of loneliness and finds it hard to fit in with the locals.

In order to impress, she enters the annual Great Quiche Competition. Never having cooked a quiche in her life, she cheats by buying one from a swanky store in London. But when the competition judge drops dead, Agatha's lie is exposed and her status in the village sinks even lower. She decides she must turn amateur sleuth to save her name.

VICTIMS

Major Cummings-Browne: retired army type and a boorish freeloader. After he and his wife rip Agatha off by accepting an expensive meal, he is found dead, poisoned by a deadly plant called cowbane which is hidden in Agatha's quiche.

BOOK 2:
Agatha Raisin and the Vicious Vet

Agatha's flirtation with the good-looking new vet in the village is cut short by his untimely demise, prompting her to take up her second case as an amateur detective. Paul Bladen was murdered with his own syringe of horse tranquillizer as he prepared to perform an operation on Lord Pendlebury's prize racehorse. The police are keen to write it off as a tragic accident, but Agatha and neighbour James Lacey suspect foul play.

Their investigations lead them to the discovery that the vet was busy romancing half the women in the village with the aim of extracting money from them, apparently to feed his gambling habit. After a local villager summons Agatha to tell her what she knows about the murder, she is also found dead.

After her cats are kidnapped, Agatha puts her own life at risk to rescue them and nail the murderer.

VICTIMS

Paul Bladen: dishy vet, womanizer and extortionist, murdered with an injection of horse medication after being hit over the head while operating on Lord Pendlebury's racehorse.

Mrs Josephs: a pleasant librarian and member of Carsely Ladies' Society who was heartbroken when her ancient cat was put down by the vet without consultation. Found dead in her bathroom, killed by an injection of adrenalin.

BOOK 3:

Agatha Raisin and the Potted Gardener

Jealous of James Lacey's new love interest, divorcée and wizard gardener Mary Fortune, Agatha calls in Roy to provide an instant garden, pretending that her own hard work and aptitude have created the vision. She erects a huge fence around her bare garden and plans to unveil the magnificent transformation on the village open day. In return for Roy's help, she agrees to go back to PR on a temporary basis.

As the horticultural show approaches, a series of petty crimes are committed against the contenders, including the trampling of Mrs Mason's prize dahlias, a hole dug in Miss Simms' lawn and James's roses being torched. Mary comes under suspicion.

After the show, James and Agatha discover Mary 'planted' head down in a flowerpot, with her legs suspended from hooks in the ceiling. Dressed, as she always was, in green, she resembles a potted plant.

After James confesses to an affair with her, the pair set about trying to find a green-fingered murderer with a reason to kill Mary.

VICTIM

Mary Fortune: glamorous divorcée recently moved into the village. Elegant and attractive, she is an instant hit with the villagers and James. Poisoned with a drugged brandy and then planted among her prized tropical plants.

BOOK 4:

Agatha Raisin and the Walkers of Dembley

Agatha returns from her stint in London, working for the PR firm she sold her business to, and finds James running a local ramblers' club. In order to lose weight, and get closer to her attractive neighbour, she signs up for the walks. In the nearby town of Dembley, the formidable leader of the local ramblers' association declares war on local baronet, Sir Charles Fraith, and vows to cross his land using an ancient right of way. Jessica Tartinck's body is found, a few days later, in the middle of Sir Charles's rape field and he is arrested. Agatha is asked to investigate by Carsely neighbour, Mrs Mason, whose niece, a Dembley rambler, had recently started dating Sir Charles. To find out who the killer is, Agatha and James pose as man and wife and hole up in a flat in Dembley,

joining the Ramblers' Association and discovering a whole raft of suspects with a motive to kill Jessica.

Their enforced living arrangements at first drive James and Agatha further apart, but the starchy historian springs a welcome surprise on her at the end of the book.

VICTIMS

Jessica Tartinck: militant leader of the Dembley Walkers and ex-Greenham Common campaigner. Determined to march across the rape field on Sir Charles Fraith's land, she took umbrage when the charming aristocrat won over the rest of the group and went alone. Killed by a blow to the back of the head with a spade and then buried in a field.

Jeffrey Benson: Jessica's lover, fellow rambler and former IRA sympathizer. Murdered with a blow to the head as he cut the padlock on a landowner's gate.

BOOK 5:

Agatha Raisin and the Murderous Marriage

At last, Agatha has her man but life is not all rosy in the garden just yet. As she goes about making her wedding plans, she is fully aware that she never divorced her alcoholic ex, Jimmy Raisin, and has lied to James, telling him that her first husband died of drink

years ago. Aware she has no proof that this is the case, and terrified to delay the nuptials in case she loses the love of her life, Agatha opts to get married in the registry office instead of the village church, upsetting her friend, Mrs Bloxby, as well as many of the villagers.

In her typically insensitive way, Agatha also manages to upset her young friend Roy, who worked for her in the PR firm she owned and stayed with the company when she sold it. After he is not given credit for his help in one of her murder enquiries, Roy takes offence and, in a fit of pique, hires a private detective to track down the errant ex. As a blissful Agatha prepares to become Mrs Lacey, the wedding is halted by local policeman Fred Griggs, who has met Jimmy in the village and discovered that Agatha is about to commit bigamy. Faced with Jimmy, Agatha screams, 'I'll kill you, you bastard,' in front of the gathered guests. A furious James tells her she has disgraced him and he will never forgive her. Devastated, she pays Jimmy to go away and retires to her empty home to lick her wounds. As dawn breaks the following day, Agatha ventures out, only to be confronted by her drunken ex who she shoves into a ditch, screeching, 'Why don't you die?'

When Jimmy is found dead in the same ditch, less than an hour later, Agatha is charged with his murder. Having sold her house, she has nowhere to go until James returns and offers her his spare room. Together they set out to find the real murderer and clear their own names as several more victims fall along the

way. And while all roads seem to lead to a Mrs Serena Gore-Appleton, who had attended a health farm with Jimmy, the mysterious lady seems impossible to track down.

VICTIMS

Jimmy Raisin: Agatha's drunken ex-husband, strangled with his own tie a short time after Agatha's assault on him.

Janet Purvey: a local spinster, who had attended the health farm at the same time as Jimmy and the elusive Mrs Gore-Appleton. Claimed Jimmy had 'come on' to her. Strangled by someone she vaguely recognized as she watched *Die Hard* in Mircester's cinema.

Sir Desmond Derrington: married aristocrat who was being blackmailed by Jimmy over the mistress he had taken to the health farm. Shot himself after a visit from Agatha and James as he feared his affair would be exposed to his wife.

Helen Warwick: House of Commons secretary and lover of Sir Desmond. Agatha's hackles rose when she took a shine to James, but he soon realized she was a gold-digger. Murdered with her own scarf after turning up in Carsely to see James but not finding him at home.

BOOK 6:

Agatha Raisin and the Terrible Tourist

After the aborted nuptials, James has fled to Northern Cyprus and Agatha decides to follow him there. Before she tracks him down, however, she takes a boat trip and meets two parties of holidaymakers – a snooty couple called the Debenhams, with an equally upper-class friend, and the Wilcoxes, a seemingly wealthy, lower-class couple also accompanied by an elderly family friend.

Finally she tracks James down to the villa he rented for their honeymoon, which is in an appalling state. The following day he rents a new villa and, at the suggestion of the locals showing them round, Agatha opts to share with him. At dinner that night, they are press-ganged into joining the group from the boat trip, who have now joined forces, and go on to a nightclub. There, a drunken Rose Wilcox slides under the table and is soon found to have been murdered. Agatha is forced to stay on the island until the murderer is found.

By coincidence, Sir Charles Fraith arrives at the Dome Hotel and takes Agatha out for the evening. Although she is still in love with James, Agatha ends up sleeping with him in his hotel room.

VICTIMS

Rose Wilcox: blowzy British tourist married to self-made businessman Trevor. Sexy and flirty, but clearly hiding her true intelligence
under a dumb exterior. Murdered in the nightclub in Cyprus with
a long, sharp blade in the back.

Harry Tembleton: older friend of upper-class couple, Olivia and
George Debenham. Found by Agatha, dead on the beach with his
face covered by a newspaper, having been murdered with a similar
weapon to that used on Rose.

BOOK 7:
Agatha Raisin and the Wellspring of Death

A penitent Roy Silver persuades Agatha back into PR, to
represent a local mineral water company. They are keen to exploit
a natural spring in the village of Ancombe, next to Carsely, but
the villagers are divided over the scheme. As the debate rages on,
Robert Struthers, the chairman of the parish council, is found
dead by the spring. Although he was undecided on the issue, it
looks like someone has silenced him before he had a chance to
cast the deciding vote. Agatha must now investigate the parish
council and solve the murder, while promoting the water
company in the wake of a scandal.

Still smarting from her disastrous relationship with James,

Agatha dates Guy Freemont, who owns Ancombe Water Company with his brother Peter. Meanwhile, James goes for a radical makeover – dyed-blond hair, three earrings, dirty jeans and boots – to infiltrate an environmental group called Save Our Foxes, determined to carry out his own independent investigation.

VICTIMS

Robert Struthers: chairman of Ancombe Parish Council, and undecided on the issue of the spring. Hit on the head and left lying at the spring, with blood seeping into the water. The body is found by Agatha as she walks to Ancombe one evening.

Robina Toynbee: owner of the spring. Received death threats after selling the water to the company, but dismissed them as crank letters from militant environmentalists. Found hanging upside down from her garden wall, with blood gushing from her head into the spring, during a procession with a marching band organized by Agatha.

BOOK 8:

Agatha Raisin and the Wizard of Evesham

With James and Charles away, and Bill on holiday, Agatha is depressed and lonely.

Following the horrifying discovery of grey hairs, she attempts

to tint her hair and instead turns it purple. On Mrs Bloxby's recommendation, she seeks help from a talented hairdresser called Mr John, who has a salon in Evesham. Flattered by the good-looking crimper, she agrees to a date, but when she sees the frightened face of a lady they bump into in the restaurant, she becomes suspicious of her new admirer. In an attempt to discover whether he is a blackmailer, she has dinner with him again and begins to fall for his charms. While she is on a visit to his salon, however, he begins to vomit and dies.

Unwilling to drop the case, Agatha decides to break into his house to find out what he was hiding but, while she searches in the basement, the building is set alight and she narrowly escapes through a window. But who wanted the popular hairdresser dead?

VICTIMS

John Shawpart: the Wizard of Evesham. Brilliant and attractive hairdresser who preyed on vulnerable women using flattery and then blackmail. Poisoned by a ricin injection in a vitamin capsule.

Mrs Darry: Carsely villager and incorrigible gossip who was detested by Agatha. Had been blackmailed by John over tax evasion and later killed with a poker in her own home. The body was found by Agatha and Charles alongside the corpse of her dog.

Agatha Raisin
COMPANION

BOOK 9:

Agatha Raisin and the Witch of Wyckhadden

After a run-in with a psychopathic hairdresser, who used depilatory cream on her glossy brown hair rather than conditioner, Agatha flees to the seaside town of Wyckhadden to allow it grow back away from the gaze of the villagers and, particularly, James Lacey. There she meets local police chief Jimmy Jessop, a widower, and a romance develops.

In an effort to help her hair grow back, she visits the resident witch, who gives her a restorative lotion as well as a love potion. But after her prized fur coat is vandalized at the hotel, Agatha suspects the witch and returns to confront her, only to find her dead in a pool of blood. Forced to stay in the town, she slips a love potion into Jimmy's drink and ends up sleeping with him. He asks her to marry him and she accepts, all the while imagining the effect her engagement will have on James.

She also slips some of the potion into the drink of a retired colonel, resident at the hotel, hoping he will fall for a lovesick fellow guest. When he dies from natural causes, the distraught admirer throws herself from a window.

When Sir Charles Fraith arrives on the scene, an upset Agatha welcomes him with open arms – and ends up sleeping with him too. James Lacey also turns up at the hotel, at the same time as Jimmy walks in on his new fiancée, still in bed with Charles.

VICTIMS

Francie Juddle, the Witch of Wyckhadden: beaten to death with a large, heavy object in her own bed. Found by Agatha after supplying her with a lotion to make her hair grow.

Janine Juddle: Francie's daughter who arrives in Wyckhadden with her husband and takes over her mother's business. Drowns after arranging a seance attended by most of the residents of the Garden Hotel, where Agatha is staying. Professes to have conjured up the ghost of Jimmy Raisin but Agatha catches her out. Found by the residents floating in the sea shortly afterwards.

BOOK 10:
Agatha Raisin and the Fairies of Fryfam

Following the ill-advised liaison with Charles, Jimmy Jessop has found a new bride and James Lacey has once more fled Carsely, leaving Agatha alone again. Sick of the Cotswolds and her roller coaster of emotions, she consults a fortune teller who assures her that her destiny lies in Norfolk. She immediately puts her house up for sale and rents a cottage in the Norfolk village of Fryfam, picked by sticking a pin in a map.

After taking against a couple who come to view the house, she changes her mind about selling, but decides to spend some time in Norfolk anyway. Ensconced in Lavender Cottage with her

cats, amid a local population of rude villagers with archaic views on women, Agatha decides to try her hand at writing a detective novel.

Every evening, however, she is disturbed by tiny lights flickering at the bottom of her garden, which the more super-stitious locals believe to be fairies. When objects begin to go missing from her house, Agatha wonders if the villagers are playing tricks on her. But events take a sinister turn when a valuable Stubbs is stolen from the lord of the manor, who is later murdered. With the help of Charles, who turns up at the cottage unannounced, Agatha uncovers a seam of blackmail, adultery and jealousy in the close-knit community.

Meanwhile, in Carsely, James is being pursued by another attractive divorcée – but is he pining for Agatha?

VICTIMS

Terence 'Tolly' Trumpington-James: self-styled lord of the manor who made his money from installing showers. After his priceless painting disappears, he is found at his huge stately home, with his throat slit.

Paul Redfern: gruff, aggressive gamekeeper at the manor. His head is blown off with a shotgun in his grace-and-favour cottage. His body is discovered by Sir Charles and Agatha when they turn up to question him about Tolly's death.

BOOK 11.

Agatha Raisin and the Love from Hell

The life that Agatha dreamed of has turned into a nightmare. Now married to the love of her life, she is trapped in a 'fog of masculine disapproval'. James criticizes everything she does and, as soon as the honeymoon is over, he turns into a control freak, constantly telling her what to wear and do. When she decides to take a PR job for a local shoe firm, James is furious, but she presses ahead anyway.

Finding him in a pub with divorcée Melissa Sheppard, Agatha flies into a jealous rage, but when Sir Charles comes to visit her in her own cottage, James assumes she is the one who is cheating. In the meantime, James has confided in Mrs Bloxby that he has a brain tumour but doesn't want to tell his new wife. After their reconciliation, Agatha learns the truth about his illness from Melissa but, before she can confront him, he disappears, leaving behind signs of a violent struggle in his house. Agatha is suspected of his murder until the discovery of his lover's body turns the suspicion on to him.

With Charles's help, Agatha must find her missing husband and clear both their names. She soon discovers Melissa's two ex-husbands, a love rival and a jealous sister – all with a motive for murder.

Agatha Raisin
COMPANION

VICTIM

Melissa Sheppard, two-time divorcée and lover of James. Her head is bashed in at her kitchen table and the fly-infested body is found nearly two days later by Agatha and Charles.

BOOK 12:
The Day the Floods Came

Agatha is once more abandoned, with James having fled to live in a monastery and Charles settling down, at last, with a French girl in Paris. She takes a break on Robinson Crusoe Island in South America, where she meets a group of people, including a newly-wed couple who make her feel uneasy.

On her return home, she learns that the bride drowned shortly after, and she suspects the young groom of pushing her in the sea. A few months later, the Avon floods its banks and Agatha, standing on a bridge in Evesham, spots the body of a bride-to-be floating in the swollen river. Police rule it a suicide, but convinced that it was the bridegroom, yet again, she sets about solving the case. As the police have warned her off, she invests in a wig and poses as a TV producer researching a programme.

In Carsely, James's cottage is sold to a crime writer named John Armitage who happens to be single and extremely attractive. He begins to help Agatha with her investigation.

VICTIMS

Concita Ramon: newlywed who was spending her honeymoon on Robinson Crusoe Island. Not being able to swim, she drowned on a boat trip and husband Pablo claimed she fell in. He was spotted pushing his heavily insured bride into the sea.

Kylie Stokes: admin clerk and bride-to-be. Drowned in the flood water after being pumped full of drugs. Agatha suspects her fiancé, who runs a club with his dad, but police believe it is a suicide.

Mrs Anstruther-Jones: Carsely villager and member of the Ladies' Society. Killed by a hit and run driver in Evesham after borrowing Agatha's wig and glasses for a secret liaison with a married man. Mistaken for Agatha by the killer.

Joanna Field: colleague of Kylie who takes a shine to John and agrees to help them. Smacked on the back of the head as she looks through Kylie's emails, but survives. Later she goes missing and is found with her neck broken in an old freezer room behind the nightclub.

BOOK 13:

Agatha Raisin and the Curious Curate

Agatha discovers that ex-husband James has left the monastery without taking holy orders, leaving her feeling even more rejected. Still smarting from John Armitage's ungallant proposition, she falls hook, line and sinker for the beautiful young curate, Tristan. She is thrilled when he invites her for dinner in his digs, but on the same night he is stabbed at the vicarage and dies, apparently while raiding the collection box.

Along with John Armitage, Agatha investigates at his old parish, New Cross, where they discover he was gay and that he had conned a donation of £10,000 from philanthropic tycoon Richard Binser for a fictional boys' club.

It seems the curate was not the quite the golden boy he appeared to be.

VICTIMS

Tristan Delon: blond-haired, blue-eyed and beautiful, he has the ladies of the parish eating out of his hand. Stabbed to death in the vicar's study, with the vicar's letter-opener, in the middle of the night. Found by Mrs Bloxby in the morning.

Miss Jellop: thin, middle-aged Carsely resident and member of the Ladies' Society who Tristan had been spending time with.

Strangled in her home and discovered, once again, by the vicar's wife as she called round.

Peggy Slither: another middle-aged lady who Tristan wooed with an eye to getting his hands on her money. Stabbed to death in a gory murder in her Ancombe home. This time the body was found by Agatha.

BOOK 14:

Agatha Raisin and the Haunted House

With no murders on the horizon, Agatha gets involved in investigating a haunted house at the behest of her new neighbour, the attractive Paul Chatterton. She proves fairly inept at dealing with the supernatural, as the sight of the old lady who lives there, wearing a facepack, sends her screaming from the house.

But old Mrs Witherspoon is murdered soon after their visit. Her son is the prime suspect and Agatha and Paul are asked to prove him innocent. They discover a secret tunnel to Mrs Witherspoon's house and a priceless manuscript hidden in a hole up a vent, which they decide to keep from the police.

The case is further complicated when a second victim is murdered in the dressing room of her amateur dramatic theatre.

VICTIMS

Mrs Witherspoon: crotchety, vicious old lady despised by her own children. After months of being 'haunted', she is whacked on the back of the head and dies as she falls down the stairs.

Robin Barley: smart, wealthy woman in her sixties who fancies herself an artist, although she has little talent. She owns the local theatre, which ensures her a part in the amateur plays there. Killed by cyanide in her roses, delivered by an anonymous 'admirer' in a gas mask, the costume from the next production of *Macbeth*.

Barry Briar: landlord of the local pub in Hebberden, the village where Mrs Witherspoon was murdered. After going missing for several days, his body, with a broken neck, is discovered at the bottom of a shaft which leads to the secret tunnel. Agatha, accompanied by Charles, finds him after a nightmare prompts her to look there.

BOOK 15:

Agatha Raisin and the Deadly Dance

After a dreadful time in Paris, where she is robbed on the Metro and then dismissed by the police, Agatha decides to open her own detective agency. An advert for a secretary brings in her new neighbour, Mrs Emma Comfrey, who has taken over James's cottage. She soon passes Agatha's test by finding a missing cat in record time, and is employed as a detective. But a lunch date with Sir Charles leads to an unhealthy obsession.

In her first real case, Agatha is hired by upper-class Lady of the Manor, Catherine Laggatt-Brown, who fears for her daughter's life. Cassandra is about to announce her engagement at a dinner dance thrown for her twenty-first birthday, but has received a death threat saying that if she marries her boyfriend, Jason, she will die. The occasion is ruined when a sniper takes a pot-shot at the birthday girl and Agatha pushes her and her mother into the swimming pool to save their lives.

As the case progresses, it appears Cassandra isn't the only one whose life is in danger.

VICTIMS

Harrison Peterson: groom-to-be Jason's father, an ex-con. He is found dead in his lodgings by Agatha and Patrick, who want to ask him questions about the gunshot. After finding an empty

bottle of pills and a bottle of vodka, police assume it is suicide but it is later discovered to be murder.

The hitman: a trained assassin sent to dispatch Agatha. Instead, he picks a night when she is in Paris with Charles, drinks poisoned coffee intended for Agatha, and is found dead in her kitchen with a gun still in his hands.

Emma Comfrey: Agatha's neighbour and colleague in the detective agency. Shot in the head by the murderer who mistakes her for Agatha in the kitchen of the latter's Carsely cottage.

BOOK 16:
Agatha Raisin and the Perfect Paragon

With the detective agency booming, Agatha is persuaded by Mrs Bloxby to take on ageing local photographer Phil. The seventy-six-year-old camera expert promises to bring her a new case, and introduces her to Robert Smedley, who believes his wife Mabel is cheating. Finding little evidence of that, Agatha switches her attention to the case of missing teenager Jessica Bradley, who disappeared after leaving a Mircester nightclub without her two pals, Trixie and Fairy. With excellent powers of deduction, Phil helps his new boss find the body of the murdered sixteen-year-old, dumped in the woods near a road. Wallowing in the

publicity, Agatha promises to find the murderer for free. She soon uncovers the seedy secret of the three teenage girls and when Smedley is murdered, followed by Jessica's much older boyfriend, it begins to look as if the three are connected.

Meanwhile, Agatha employs bright eighteen-year-old goth Harry Beam and persuades ex-policeman Patrick, who is already divorcing the flighty Miss Simms, to return to the agency. She also comes to the rescue of her old friend Roy, sacked for giving an ill-advised interview about a rock band's drug habit to the *Daily Mail.* Her obsession with James Lacey is forgotten when she meets Charles's handsome pal Freddy, but will he get round to telling her he is married?

VICTIMS

Jessica Bradley: sixteen-year-old student murdered on her way home from the Happy Night Club. Possibly picked up by a car, she was stabbed and her body was dumped by the side of the dual carriageway. Her clothing was removed to make it look like rape, but the police examination reveals she was a virgin.

Robert Smedley: Ancombe businessman who runs an electronics company owned by his wife. He hires Agatha to find out if Mabel was cheating but, after withdrawing his case, is found poisoned in his office. He was having an affair with his secretary, Joyce, who is now a suspect.

Burt Haviland: Jessica's much older boyfriend, who worked for Smedley at the electronics firm. He has a conviction for armed robbery and is behind the soft porn website which showed intimate films of Jessica, Trixie and Fairy. Stabbed in his own flat.

BOOK 17:

Agatha Raisin and Love, Lies and Liquor

Having made a surprise return in *Perfect Paragon*, James moves back into the cottage next to Agatha's and invites her to a barbecue. Snubbed by the guests and ignored by James, Agatha storms out and vows never to have anything more to do with him. Eventually, a chastened James wins her round with the promise of a mystery holiday, but Agatha's dreams of Mediterranean sunshine are dashed when they end up in the wet and windy seaside town of Snoth-on-Sea.

The holiday goes from bad to worse when a honeymooning guest, who Agatha and James had argued with in the dining room, is found strangled on the beach – and Agatha's scarf is identified as the murder weapon. Agatha is keen to get to the bottom of the mystery but, after another quarrel, James flees to France.

Agency employees Patrick and Harry join Agatha in the hotel to help out and Sir Charles also sails to her side after yet another broken romance.

VICTIMS

Geraldine Jankers: newly wed to the cowed Fred, her fourth husband, and honeymooning with her yobby son Wayne and his wife Chelsea, as well as family friends Cyril and Dawn Hammond. Strangled with Agatha's scarf in the middle of the night after slipping out while her husband slept.

Wayne and Chelsea Weldon: chavvy son from Geraldine's first marriage and his young wife. Wayne picked a fight with James on their first night, but came off worse. Found in their hotel room with shotgun wounds after Chelsea showed off a diamond necklace at the resort.

Deborah Fanshawe: attractive Carsely divorcee who was chasing James and then Charles. Mistaken for Agatha and shot in the head as she waited in her love rival's hotel room.

BOOK 18:

Agatha Raisin and Kissing Christmas Goodbye

With James abroad and the detective agency turning over a steady stream of missing pets and divorce cases, Agatha is so bored that she starts dreaming of Christmas – in October.

To break the monotony, she accepts the case of a wealthy

woman who believes she will soon be murdered. Phyllis Tamworthy lives in a stately manor house in the village of Lower Tapor, which she also owns. Preparing to celebrate her birthday with her four children and other family members, she tells Agatha she is about to change her will and very little of her vast wealth will be going to her offspring. As a result she reveals that she expects someone has murder in mind and asks Agatha to attend the party. The detective's presence, with Sir Charles, is not enough to prevent her hostess being poisoned and Agatha is soon investigating which of the money-grabbing siblings is most likely to have done the deed.

When her latest recruit, seventeen-year-old Toni, stumbles upon a witchcraft meeting in the village, the case takes on a spookier side.

VICTIMS

Phyllis Tamworthy: rich but common lady of the manor and graceless mother, grandmother and great-grandmother. After serving up her own special salad at the family gathering she collapses and later dies, poisoned by hemlock. All four children stood to lose their inheritance when she changed her will the following week.

Fred Instick: ancient gardener on the Tamworthy estate who lives in a rundown cottage on the land. Poisoned with hemlock in a bottle of wine stolen from

the kitchen of the house after he told the family he knew who murdered Phyllis.

Paul Chambers: pub landlord in Lower Tapor who attempted to rape Toni. Pushed into a quarry by furious girlfriend Elsie, after he refused to marry her during a naked witchcraft ritual. Death seemingly unconnected to the original murders.

Susan Mason: work colleague and lover of Phyllis's late husband, disappeared fifty-eight years ago in the Tamworthys' old home village of Pirdey, near Stoke on Trent, shortly after Hugh had said he wanted to marry her. Toni finds the body buried underneath the outhouse at the couple's former home after acting on a hunch.

Jimmy Tamworthy: originally thought to have been murdered in an occult ceremony, but it soon emerges that he hanged himself.

BOOK 19:
Agatha Raisin and a Spoonful of Poison

Our heroine is asked, by her close friend Mrs Bloxby, to use her PR skills to help a vicar in a neighbouring village raise money at the annual fête. Agatha is reluctant until she meets the vicar, and his extremely attractive widowed friend George Selby. To impress, she cajoles a singing superstar into opening the fête and

raises £30,000. But in the jam-tasting tent, the local preserves have been laced with LSD and the resulting chaos results in the untimely deaths of two of the parishioners.

Hired by the vicar to investigate the crime, Agatha is only too pleased to help – especially if it means spending more time with gorgeous George.

VICTIMS

Mrs Andrews: elderly lady from the village of Comfrey Magna. After sampling the jam, she jumps from the bell tower of the church, believing she could fly, and is killed on the tombstone below.

Mrs Jessop: another local victim of the poisoned preserves. As the fête is still going on, she jumps in the river and drowns.

Sarah Selby: George's pretty wife, who was found dead at their home long before the jam incident, having fallen down the stone stairs. Local toff Sybilla, who was infatuated with George, was there at the time and local gossips link her to the death.

Sybilla Triast-Perkins: local lady of the manor, who apparently hanged herself in her hallway and was found by Agatha and Roy. Her suicide note mentioned her guilt over 'a death', but was she referring to the LSD disaster or the death of Sarah Selby?

Arnold Birntweather: church accountant who was charged with looking after the cash from the successful fête. Murdered with a savage blow to the head after taking the cash out of the bank, seemingly under pressure.

BOOK 20:
Agatha Raisin: There Goes the Bride

Smarting from James's engagement to the stunning Felicity, Agatha has thrown herself into work and, suffering from stress and exhaustion, taken a tumble on the stairs. Her friends urge her to have a break and she chooses a trip to Istanbul, incorporating some excursions to historic battle sites, so that she can later impress James with her knowledge. When James and his fiancée turn up in the same place as her, twice, he is convinced she is stalking him.

On the day of the wedding, the bride is murdered and Agatha and James are chief suspects. But the family, believing her to be innocent, employ her to find the real killer – until she begins to discover a past they would rather keep hidden.

VICTIMS

Felicity Bross-Tilkington: James's bride-to-be, only daughter of a rich

couple who made their money in Spanish property. A reputed nymphomaniac, engaged twice before, she gave regular peep shows to the local lads but played the virgin with her fiancé. Shot on the morning of the wedding as she dressed in the bedroom.

Sean Fitzpatrick: Irish boatsman and odd job man who helped out the Bross-Tilkingtons occasionally. Agatha finds him dead on his boat when she goes to talk to him. He has been shot. Police uncover links with the IRA.

Bert Trymp: local mechanic who also owns a boat in the marina. He telephones Agatha and invites her round because he had information relating to Sean's murder. Charles and Agatha later find his body floating in the river at the bottom of Bross-Tilkington's estate.

George Bross-Tilkington: Felicity's father, a rich businessman who made his money in foreign property. He is blown up in a boat in Spain.

6
Close Shaves

Agatha's line of work inevitably puts her in a dangerous position and she has survived numerous attempts on her life. She has been drugged, hit over the head and held at gunpoint but, through a combination of chutzpah, sheer bloody-mindedness and the 'luck of the devil', she has so far lived to fight on.

Quiche of Death

After receiving a misspelt death threat, Agatha is brought off her bicycle by a wire stretched across the road on the steep hill into Carsely. Bill Wong pulls up as her attacker is about to finish the job with a large rock. Later, she is drugged with sleeping pills and left in a burning house. She is once again saved by Bill, who manages to push her out of a broken window.

Vicious Vet

The murderer attempts to kill Agatha with a shotgun, but is foiled when her beloved cat, Hodge, jumps on his face. She hears another gunshot and waits for the worst, but when she opens her eyes, it is the killer who has shot himself.

Murderous Marriage

Petrol is poured through the letterbox of James's cottage where Agatha is staying. The couple throw water at the flames and Mrs Hardy, who has bought Agatha's house, comes to the rescue with buckets of earth. Later, Agatha, James and Mrs Hardy are accosted by a masked gunman while walking home from the village dance and the sour-faced neighbour comes to the rescue once more, kicking the gun from his hand. Finally the real murderer, who Agatha has uncovered, smacks her over the head with a brass poker and attempts to bury her alive in her own garden, but she is rescued by Fred Griggs and Bill Wong.

Terrible Tourist

During the Cyprus murder mystery, there are three attempts on Agatha's life. First, she is almost pushed from the window of the monument at Saint Hilarion, in North Cyprus. Secondly, a rock is thrown at her head as she gets in a car, and finally the perpetrator attempts to smother her in a room at the Dome Hotel. Agatha fights her attacker off, but is left shaken and sick by the ordeal.

Wellspring of Death

The murderer holds Agatha and Mrs Bloxby at gunpoint and forces them to drive away from Carsely towards Stratford. After they stop in a field, Agatha sprays hairspray into the villain's eyes and brave Mrs Bloxby shoots him in the chest.

Wizard of Evesham

Agatha is attacked by the murderer, who repeatedly bangs her head against the wash basin as she is having her hair done. She is saved by Charles, who calls the police.

Fairies of Fryfam

Agatha is threatened with a shotgun in her rented cottage and is saved when Charles spots the open door and the frightened cats and calls the police.

Day the Floods Came

A hit and run attempt is foiled when Agatha spots the car approaching and throws herself over a garden hedge. Later, however, Mrs Anstruther-Jones is killed by the same method, while wearing Agatha's disguise. Agatha also finds herself locked in a freezer storage room behind a nightclub, and is rescued by John Armitage, Mrs Bloxby and her surly husband, Alf.

Curious Curate

After meeting the person she suspected to be the killer at home, Agatha is asked to look at the wine cellar. As she peers down the stone steps, she is hit on the back of the head with a heavy object and tumbles down. Tied up at the bottom of the stairs, Agatha hears policemen come to the door and take the killer away for questioning, but is sure he or she will return to finish her off. Alerted by John, however, Bill Wong sounds the alarm and the police rescue Agatha.

Haunted House

The killer confronts Agatha and Charles in the living room of her cottage and threatens them with a gun. He promises to start at the kneecaps and keep shooting until they tell him what he wants to know but, alerted to his presence in the next-door cottage, she has already phoned Bill Wong. The police arrive just in time.

Deadly Dance

Used to being the target of murderers, in this complicated case

Agatha finds herself in the sights of two potential killers. A jealous neighbour's attempts to finish her off only serve to thwart a professional assassin who has been hired by someone else. When he is found dead in the kitchen, the real killer comes to the cottage, armed and dangerous, and instead murders the psychopathic neighbour.

Love, Lies and Liquor

Charmed by a mysterious stranger called Terry Armstrong, Agatha agrees to a date. Her suitor offers to drive her out of the oppressive surrounds of Snoth-on-Sea to a nice restaurant, but stops en route at an abandoned building where he forces her in at gunpoint. She is saved after Patrick calls the police, suspecting the man's motives. He turns out to be drug baron Brian McNally, who is after the missing jewels from a bank robbery involving the ex of murder victim Geraldine Jankers.

Carsely woman Deborah Fanshawe is later shot while waiting in Agatha's hotel room, in a clear case of mistaken identity, and Agatha is almost killed again when Brian McNally cons his way into the Grand by pretending to be a CID officer. As he points his gun at her, a wave crashes through the lounge window and saves her.

Kissing Christmas Goodbye

The murderer attempts to poison Agatha's toothpaste by injecting

hemlock into the tube. Warned by a concerned Mrs Bloxby, Agatha spies on her in the bathroom and sees her doctoring the tube. After she confronts her, the murderer attacks, but is pulled off by Bill Wong, who has been alerted by the vicar's wife.

Spoonful of Poison

Punched in the face by the very man she had almost fallen for, Agatha is saved by Mrs Bloxby, who attacks him with a jar of chutney. She is then targeted by the killer, who poisons the milk on her doorstep. Agatha realizes what has happened when she sees a dead bird, which has pecked off the lid, thereby saving her cats from certain death. At the same time, her young detective Toni is confronted by the murderer, wielding a knife, but manages to fight her off with a chair.

There Goes the Bride

The murder of Felicity Bross-Tilkington, James's young fiancée,

proves to be one of Agatha's most perilous cases, with three attempts on her life.

While looking for clues in Barcelona, she is grabbed from behind and knocked out with chloroform. When she awakes, she is on a boat and a woman is about to inject her with a drug. She begs her not to and the lady concedes, telling Agatha to play dead. She is then bundled on to another boat and escapes into the water, shortly before the boat explodes. Back home, she joins a dating agency and arranges to meet a respectable lord at London's St Katharine's Dock, but is once more drugged and escapes death by stabbing her captor in the neck with his own hypodermic needle. A third attempt is made by a woman who befriends Agatha after bumping into her in a market. She then suggests an outing to Warwick Castle, but Agatha foils her plan to inject her by stealing her handbag.

7
A Cast of Carsely Characters

Agatha arrives in the Cotswolds without a friend in the world and finds it hard to get close to anyone, used as she is to bullying and cajoling her way through life as a PR person. Her new life brings fringe benefits as she becomes part of the village and forms some real friendships, as well as making a few acquaintances, and even a couple of enemies.

Below are the regular characters that pop up in Agatha's busy life.

Bill Wong

Agatha's very first friend in the Cotswolds, Bill is an amiable, likeable and often shrewd policeman from nearby Mircester. Agatha meets him when he comes to investigate the poisoned quiche in the first book and, from the pristine cookery books and the new cooking utensils in her kitchen, he quickly deduces that she has not baked it herself. He calls back later, unofficially, and advises her sagely that if she

wants to make her mark on the village she should 'try becoming popular'. The pair become firm friends and she is grateful for his company as she settles into her new home. Her first cat, Hodge, is an early gift from him.

Bill is twenty-three when they meet. He is small and chubby, with oriental looks which come from a father who is Hong Kong Chinese. His parents, with whom he still lives, are a particularly rude pair, with excruciatingly bad taste and little to say, but Bill adores them. His mother is also a terrible cook and Agatha dreads the invitations to dinner which her young friend often issues. Bill, who frequently falls in love, also fails to notice that it is his offensive parents that put off his potential partners. Agatha 'did not like to point out to Bill that his formidable parents could probably see off any prospect, for Bill adored his parents.'

The one girl who seems to get on with the family is Toni Gilmour, whose home life had been much worse. Unfortunately, there was no spark between the pair and they ended as friends.

Mrs Bloxby

Mrs Bloxby, the wife of Carsely vicar Alf, is a kind, generous soul and a good listener. After she invites Agatha to join the Ladies' Society, the pair become firm friends and Agatha often runs to Mrs Bloxby when she is troubled,

to pour her heart out and to be soothed by this wise woman while being indulged with some home-baked scones or teacakes.

As strident and stubborn as Agatha can be, she soon discovers that the vicar's wife is the one person that she can't say no to. Her 'simple, uncomplicated goodness' often makes the sensitive sleuth feel ashamed of her less charitable thoughts and deeds, and fills her with a 'desire to please'.

A petite, delicate woman, with brown hair and the 'sort of hands that portrait painters used to love to give their subjects', she is also the possessor of 'mild eyes' and boundless tolerance, even to those she secretly dislikes or distrusts.

As well as offering sage words of advice on Agatha's love life and perceptive views on the latest cases, Mrs Bloxby occasionally helps out in investigations. In *Love, Lies and Liquor*, for example, she drives to the Sussex coast to support her friend and ends up calling on suspect Archie Swale in an attempt to gain an insight into his character.

Although she is happy to listen to Agatha's troubles, she doesn't approve of her friend's obsession with James, who she believes is too cold to ever truly reciprocate.

Alf Bloxby

Mrs Bloxby's husband and Carsely's vicar. A small, thin man with a 'compelling presence', he is no fan of the village sleuth and calls her 'that dreadful woman'. He resents her frequent trips to the

vicarage to see his wife, but Mrs Bloxby handles his rude objections with tolerant good nature.

Doris Simpson

Kind, shrewd and efficient, cleaner Mrs Simpson is an invaluable help to the housework-phobic detective. She is also a great source of information, picked up through village gossip, and a shrewd judge of character.

Doris has white hair, worn in a bun, and pale grey eyes, and looks 'more like a schoolteacher than a charwoman'. Happily married to Bert, and living on the council estate in Carsely, she takes in Scrabble the cat when Agatha rescues him from Wyckhadden.

Agatha meets Doris shortly after moving to Carsely, having been told by her acerbic neighbour Mrs Barr that good cleaners are like gold dust, and Doris is too busy to help. Characteristically, Agatha sets out to steal her services by offering Doris a pound an hour more and including lunch. Of course, she succeeds.

As well as cleaning the cottage, Doris also looks after Agatha's cats on the frequent occasions that she is away.

Roy Silver

Although Roy is Agatha's former assistant and the only friend she has from her London days, they really only became close when she moved away. Roy is slim, young, camp and often selfish, using Agatha's home as a weekend getaway, popping down to pick her brains on a PR problem, or lure her back into work to further his own career. Although they weren't close when they worked together, Agatha and Roy bond when he helps her on several cases and she begins to enjoy his visits much more. His way-out clothing style changes drastically, depending on his current client, and can go from full-out punk to respectable businessman in a flash. Roy possesses a cackling laugh and a wicked sense of humour, which often leaves his older friend blushing with embarrassment.

PC Fred Griggs

Carsely's local bobby is a fat, jolly man who loves to patrol the village on foot, rather than in his car, so he can chat to people. 'He looked like a village policeman in a children's story, large and red-faced.'

Fred has little to do with investigating the murders in the area, other than being first on the scene when the crime is reported, and is 'unused to dealing with much more than looking for stolen cars in the tourist season and charging the odd drunk driver'. Nonetheless, his presence as a policeman is sorely missed after he retires and Agatha mourns the loss of the local bobby and believes crime in the country has soared.

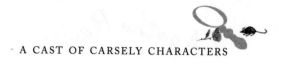

Detective Chief Inspector Wilkes

Bill Wong's boss and something of a nemesis to Agatha. He refuses to admit that she has helped his inquiries in any way, and often warns her off cases and scolds her for sticking her nose in. He is a 'thin, cadaverous man' with little sense of humour.

Carsely Ladies' Society

Although the genteel company of the Carsely Ladies' Society is anathema to the brash businesswoman in Agatha, she agrees to join through respect for Mrs Bloxby. An old-fashioned group, they never call each other by their first names, preferring instead full titles, such as Mrs Raisin. They meet regularly at the vicarage and organize village fundraising events and good works, such as taking elderly neighbours for a day out. Agatha is often roped in to run tea stalls and help out at fêtes and, on one memorable occasion, she is duped into driving the village's most unsavoury couple, the Boggles, over to Bath for the day. Agatha is at her best and most useful, however, when she is using her PR skills to boost the profits at the events and gain maximum publicity.

As well as fundraising, the group often meet with Ladies' Societies from neighbouring village and towns, particularly in Ancombe. To Agatha's surprise, the first such outing she attends, expecting to be fed tea and cake, turns out to be a boozy lunch, followed by a male strip show!

Mrs Mason is chairwoman of the society when Agatha first joins (chair 'persons' do not exist in Carsely because, as Mrs Bloxby points out, once you start that sort of thing you don't know where to stop, and things like manholes would become personholes) but Mrs Bloxby is elected chairwoman in *Curious Curate*.

Mrs Mason

The chairwoman of the Society is a large, strident woman with a taste for nylon dresses. When Agatha first moves to Carsely and vows to learn to cook, Mrs Mason gives her a few lessons in the basics, although Agatha soon resorts to the microwave again. In *Walkers of Dembley*, Mrs Mason asks Agatha to help her niece, Deborah, discover the real killer of a murdered rambler and get Sir Charles off the hook.

Miss Simms

Secretary of Carsely Ladies' Society and the village's only unmarried mother. In her twenties when they first meet, the slim, pretty girl favours tiny miniskirts and very high heels at all times. She entertains a string of partners, always married and usually in a lucrative business, but gets bored easily. Eventually, she falls for Agatha's employee, Patrick, but the union is predictably brief.

Mrs Davenport

An incomer to Carsely in *Haunted House*, Mrs Davenport is an

expat who favours print dresses and hats. She is extremely nosy and disapproving of Agatha's relationships. Having presented Paul Chatterton with 'her best chocolate cake and followed it up with two jars of home-made jam', she is miffed to discover that Agatha has been spending time with him and spreads a rumour that they are having an affair. This sparks a feud between the two women.

Mrs Josephs

Local librarian who, in *Quiche of Death*, points Agatha in the direction of the killer by revealing the loan of a book on poisonous plants. Sadly, after her cat is put down unnecessarily in *Vicious Vet*, she is also found dead, the victim of a murder herself.

Mrs Darry

Nosy, gossiping busybody from London who moves into the village in *Wellspring of Death*. She has 'a face like a startled ferret', and Agatha dislikes her intensely. Constantly sticking her nose into other people's business, she delights in spreading gossip about Agatha around the village, but ends up a victim of one of the local murderers.

8
Mrs Bloxby's Words of Wisdom

'Mrs Bloxby is such a sensible, calming sort of lady,' comments Phil in *There Goes the Bride*. In fact, everybody should have a Mrs Bloxby in their life. While Agatha seems to attract chaos and turbulence, her placid friend is an oasis of calm and always has exactly the right words for each occasion. Never flustered, or too busy to help, she dispenses wisdom to all the troubled souls of the parish, along with endless cups of tea and home-made teacakes. In fact, she is considerably better at tending to the flock than her bad-tempered husband, Alf.

Here are just a few of the words of wisdom from the great lady:

> On their first meeting: 'You struck me as a lady who had never known any real love or affection. You seem to carry a weight of loneliness about with you.' *Quiche of Death*.

'No wonder the churches are empty. I find that people who go to clairvoyants and fortune-tellers lack spirituality.' *Fairies of Fryfam*.

'I have always wondered why it is when someone says something cruel or offensive, they immediately cover it up by saying "It was only a joke. Can't you take a joke?" ' To Roy after he insulted Agatha and then backtracked in *Walkers of Dembley*.

After Agatha sleeps with Guy Freemont on their second date Agatha asks her friend, 'Does that shock you?'

'No dear, but it probably shocks you. Women of our generation never got used to casual sex,' replies Mrs Bloxby. *Wellspring of Death*.

'I have observed goodness in people as well as evil. There is a bit of the divine spirit in all of us.' *Wellspring of Death*.

'Men do not like needy women. Believe me, they can smell needy across two continents.' *Day the Floods Came*.

'Remember that the person you love when you are eighteen is not the person you would love when you are, say, twenty-five.' Mrs B's advice to Toni in *Spoonful of Poison*.

'Beauty is a dangerous thing. It can slow character formation because people are always willing to credit the beautiful with character attributes they do not have.' *Curious Curate*.

'When confronted with someone who appears to be in a perpetual state of outrage, it is tempting for other people to wind them up. Besides, I have always found the most vociferous of guardians of morality on matters of sex are those who aren't getting any. Some tea?' To nosy-parker Mrs Anstruther-Jones in *Day the Floods Came*.

On James:

'Mrs Bloxby sipped her drink and looked at the flames in the hearth. She knew that Agatha had two obsessions. One was James Lacey and the other was danger. She wondered how long Agatha would last before she started stirring things up again.' *Love, Lies and Liquor*.

'Do you think you're doing the right thing? I mean, men do not like to be pursued.' As Agatha leaves for Cyprus in *Terrible Tourist.*

'I have doubts about James Lacey. He always struck me as being a rather cold, self-contained man.' *Terrible Tourist.*

'He's nice enough, I grant you, but when it comes to women he's cold and selfish.' *Fairies of Fryfam.*

'You're letting someone live rent-free in your head.' *Fairies of Fryfam.*

9
Agatha's Men

'She did not realize that the root of the problem was that she was obsessive when it came to men. Agatha was addicted to falling in love. While she was obsessive about some man, she could dream. But now, with no current obsession, when she lay down in bed at night, there seemed to be a black hole left in her head, around the edge of which swirled nagging, petty little worries.' *Perfect Paragon*.

Agatha is never happy unless she has a man to be miserable about. Her passion borders on obsession, and the very absence of a romantic target makes her more depressed than when she is lovelorn.

Although James Lacey is the object of her most enduring fixation, there have been many passing fancies to temporarily distract her from the main prize.

James Lacey
James is the true love of her life. Agatha imagined she would

never experience grand passion until the tall, dark, handsome stranger arrived in Carsely and bought the house next door to her. 'Until she had set eyes on James Lacey, she would have sworn that all her hormones had laid down and died. She felt excited, like a schoolgirl on her first date.'

Handsome enough to 'strike any middle-aged woman all of a heap', the ex-army-officer-turned-author is over six feet tall, with blue eyes and black hair, fashionably cut, and only slightly tinged with grey.

Their initial meetings, when Agatha is about to crack the case of the poisoned quiche, lead him to believe that she is completely mad. When she meets his attractive sister, Agatha initially assumes that they are an item.

As book two, *Vicious Vet*, opens, Agatha is returning from the Bahamas with a 'tan outside and a blush of shame inside'. She had spent a fortune on flattering clothes, slimmed down for a bikini, and travelled halfway across the world to find that he was nowhere to be seen. Eventually, she phones Mrs Bloxby to be told that he changed his mind at the last minute and went to stay with a friend in Egypt – after finding out that Agatha was planning a trip to Nassau.

Studiously avoiding him to start with, she feels that James becomes more interested after she has a flirtation with the local vet, who is then murdered.

In *Potted Gardener*, it's Agatha's turn to be jealous

when James is revealed to have had an affair with Mary Fortune, the beautiful divorcée who is murdered after the village horticultural show. As the pair investigate the murder of a rambler in *Walkers of Dembley*, Agatha suggests they pose as man and wife and is thrilled that 'for a brief period she was to be Mrs Lacey, albeit in name only. But who knew what delights that could lead to!' Indeed, while their brief period of cohabiting is rocky, James finally warms to her and the pair make passionate love. The next day, he pops the question for real and an ecstatic Agatha accepts.

Something of a cold fish, James never talks about his past or his feelings. Even in the run-up to their wedding, Agatha worries that she knows little about him and asks him, 'Do you love me, James?' His typically insensitive reply is, 'I'm marrying you, aren't I?' and he then tells his fiancée that she has been watching too much Oprah Winfrey. 'I'm not a talking-about-feelings person, nor do I see the need for it.'

Murderous Marriage sees Agatha's dream of happiness dashed once more when her ex-husband, Jimmy Raisin, turns up at the wedding. A horrified James, furious that Agatha had told him Jimmy was dead, says he will never forgive her. However, when Jimmy *is* killed, he does return to help her find the real murderer, thereby clearing their names.

An uneasy friendship does eventually end in marriage when Agatha returns from a long spell in Norfolk to a pining James, who proposes. The marriage is a disaster, with constant fights,

jealousy and criticism and, after developing a brain tumour, James flees to a monastery in France. Agatha pursues him there, only to be told he is taking holy orders and selling his cottage. When she discovers he has changed his mind and left the monastery, she believes his new-found religion was merely a plot to get rid of her.

After a lengthy period of absence, James makes a surprise return and moves back into the cottage next to Agatha's in *Love, Lies and Liquor*. A disastrous barbecue with his incorrigibly rude friends helps Agatha feel that she is finally over him. James, however, is never keener than when he is being snubbed, so he wins her round with a promise of a mystery holiday. When they end up in a grotty seaside town in the rain, and Agatha finds herself accused of murder, the relationship takes a turn for the worse. Once more, James leaves her in the lurch and drives to France.

By the end of *Kissing Christmas Goodbye*, Agatha appears to be genuinely over her former paramour. When he kisses her passionately at her Christmas dinner, she feels nothing and her indifference, as usual, fuels his own feelings for her. In a missive from Arles in France, he invites her to join him and even signs off, 'Miss you', but Agatha is unmoved and ignores the plea.

Although she appears to be free of her obsession, Agatha is horrified to receive an invitation to James's engagement party, barely a month after his last letter.

On the day of the wedding, however, his bride is murdered, leaving Agatha, once more, to prove that they are both innocent.

Sir Charles Fraith

Despite the fact that he is only a minor baronet, Agatha's lowly roots mean she is initially intimidated by the dapper aristocrat during the *Walkers of Dembley* case. Sir Charles lives in the vast Barfield House, 'a large building in the fake medieval style, vaguely William Morris, with mullioned windows' which is, in Charles's own words, 'hardly an architectural gem'. It stands in a thousand acres of 'good arable land' and, when they first meet, Charles is under suspicion of the murder of a rambler, killed with a spade while crossing his rape field. Agatha is asked to investigate by Deborah, his latest conquest, and gets off on the wrong foot at an awkward lunch at the house. Rattled by the surly manservant, Gustav, and put down by the elderly aunt, she insults the family and insinuates that it would suit them to accuse a farmhand. Later she tells James she thought Sir Charles 'stupid and silly', and Charles dismisses her as a 'rather odd woman with a massive chip on her shoulder'.

The relationship thaws through the intervention of James and they become closer after Agatha saves his life during an attack by the real murderer.

Sir Charles is 'a small, neat man with fine, fair hair and a mild,

sensitive face'. Eternally well-dressed in perfectly tailored suits and beautifully pressed shirts, he rarely has a hair out of place. 'Even naked, he never looked vulnerable, but as if he were wearing a neat white suit.' (*Fairies of Fryfam*)

Although he is a clever intellectual, with a First in History from Cambridge, he prefers to play the 'bluff squire type, on the hearty side, given to rather obvious jokes and puns', but he also hides a shy character, afraid to let anyone get too close to him.

An incorrigible ladies' man, Sir Charles adds Agatha to his list of conquests in *Terrible Tourist* and then becomes one of her closest friends and an occasional partner in crime detection. By the end of the Cyprus case, the pattern for their relationship is set when he rings Agatha and says, 'Bored. Let's go for dinner.' From that day forward, Charles turns up whenever he has nothing to do. He flits in and out of Agatha's life depending on his romantic situation and, as he possesses a key to the cottage, he often moves into her spare room at short notice, disappearing again every time he meets a potential lover.

Despite Agatha's usual obsessive nature, her original fling with Charles and the occasional lapses since lack passion, and she often wonders whether he cares for her at all. Whenever he is in her company, Agatha also ponders how long he will stick around. 'In the past, he had had a habit of suddenly deciding to leave her, either because he had a date or because he had become

bored. He led a self-contained, orderly bachelor life and maintained that lifestyle by doing exactly what he wanted and when he wanted to.'

A brief marriage to a French girl, in *Day the Floods Came*, leaves Charles uncharacteristically plump, with 'thinning hair and a double chin'. After leaving his wife, however, he is soon restored to the immaculate baronet he has always been and reveals that he has been getting over lung cancer, hence the thinning hair.

Paul Bladen

The new vet has the women of the village all a-flutter and, despite her crush on James, Agatha is quite taken with him herself. In his early forties, he has thick, fair hair and light-brown eyes which 'crinkled up as though against the desert sun'. Using her recently acquired cat as an excuse, Agatha dresses up to the nines to visit the surgery, only to find all the women of Carsely in the waiting room. She is delighted when he invites her out for dinner, but flees the house when things begin to get steamy between them. As the Vicious Vet's true character emerges, it seems Agatha has had a lucky escape.

Guy Freemont

Owner of the Ancombe Water Company in *Wellspring of Death*, he charms her with champagne and dinner dates while she is nursing a broken heart following the aborted wedding to James. The first

time she meets him, Agatha thinks Guy is 'beautiful'. In his mid-thirties, tall and slim with black hair, blue eyes and 'an athlete's body', he flatters the middle-aged detective with his attentions and she sleeps with him, driving James mad with jealousy.

Mr John

Stunning hairdresser who fixes a colouring problem for Agatha before asking her out for dinner. Tall, blond and 'very, very handsome', he has an easy manner and 'very bright blue eyes, startlingly blue, as blue as a kingfisher's wing'. Women adore him for his ability to transform them and his flattery, and often confide in him. After he is murdered, it transpires that he used the information to blackmail them.

Jimmy Jessop

Kindly police inspector Jimmy meets Agatha while she is holed up in the seaside town of Wyckhadden. He has 'a lugubrious face and large pale eyes under heavy lids', black hair 'like patent leather' and is 'far from an Adonis'. But his generous nature, when met with Agatha's loneliness, sparks a romance. A widower who was devoted to his wife, he is an old-fashioned gentleman who takes Agatha dancing and finally proposes to her. But their first foray into the bedroom is a disaster and, when he finds her in bed with Charles, the engagement is most definitely off. Jimmy

quickly finds a new bride and, when Agatha returns to Wyckhadden, is about to become a father.

John Armitage

A successful and very good-looking crime writer who moves into James's old cottage, next to Agatha's house, after her marriage breaks down. As a novelist, he is interested in Agatha's cases and helps her out in *Day the Floods Came* and *Curious Curate*. At the end of the first case, he makes a clumsy pass at her, assuming she is an easy woman, and Agatha is outraged. In the aftermath, she is flattered by the attentions of the new curate, murdered on the night he has dinner with her, but later discovers he was only after money. In order to save face, she gets John to pretend he is her fiancé for the duration of the case. But as soon as the murder is solved, he sells up and moves to London.

Paul Chatterton

A charming IT expert who takes over the house after John moves out. He has a shock of white hair, sparkling black eyes and a clever face, and is besieged by the village ladies as soon as he moves in. Although Agatha avoids him at first, she succumbs when he suggests investigating the haunted house in Hebberden. While watching the house from a field, Paul kisses Agatha and she, of course, falls for him. He is married to a temperamental Spanish beauty called Juanita, who chose to stay in her homeland

when he moved to Carsely. Paul goes off in a jealous huff after Charles resurfaces and stays at Agatha's house. Saved by Agatha after being locked in an Anderson shelter, he brings her flowers in the middle of the night and is attacked by his volatile wife, eventually moving back to Spain with her.

George Shelby

Handsome widower and events organizer of the Comfrey Magna fête, where the jam is laced with LSD in *Spoonful of Poison*, George is 'tall, with fair hair, a lightly tanned, handsome face, and green eyes'. Agatha is clearly more taken with him than he is with her. When she is asked to help promote the fête, and then solve the case of the drug-laced plum jam, she uses it as an excuse to spend more time with him. She soon discovers that she is competing with his late, perfect wife and that there are suspicious circumstances surrounding her death as well. After a romantic tryst is ruined by Charles, Agatha learns that her green-eyed suitor may be more interested in her purse strings than her heart strings.

Freddy Champion

Introduced to Agatha by their mutual friend, Sir Charles, Freddy is a handsome landowner who has recently been thrown out of Zimbabwe. Visiting from South Africa, he woos Agatha behind Charles's back and neglects to tell her he is married with children.

After Freddy first asks her to dinner, Agatha allows herself to be 'wrapped in rosy dreams', but the date ends in disaster when the police arrive to quiz her about a murder, and he scuttles off in a most unchivalrous manner. He later returns for another date, but Sir Charles spots the pair in a restaurant and puts Agatha straight about Freddy's marital status before she gets in too deep.

Sylvan Dubois

A suave Frenchman with grey hair and hooded eyes who Agatha meets at James's engagement party and enjoys flirting with. When she later turns up in Paris, and calls him, he is with another woman, and she returns home, feeling silly. They meet again on the eve of James's wedding in Sussex and see more of each other after the murder of the bride. Sylvan takes Agatha out for dinner and kisses her, but his habit of showing up at every crime scene begins to look a little suspicious.

Bob Jenkins

The briefest of relationships almost ends in marriage when a bruised and battered Agatha, fresh from several attempts on her life and a self-imposed retirement, meets new local Bob. He seems a nice, normal widower, and good company. Within two months, the couple are engaged and head off for a holiday in Normandy. Alarm bells start to ring when he insists she should cook the meals and clean the house they have rented. He also

suffers from mood swings. She rings Charles and asks him to rescue her and they drive off to the south of France.

Agatha has many rivals in love, and some of them come to a sticky end.

Freda Huntingdon

An attractive newcomer referred to as 'the Merry Widow' by the jealous Agatha in *Vicious Vet*, Freda has a small, pretty face, like that of an enamelled doll, large hazel eyes with (false?) eyelashes and a 'pink, painted mouth'.

Left a great deal of money by her late husband, she moves to Carsely and soon sets her sights on James. After a couple of ill-advised affairs, including vet Paul Bladen, and finding no joy with James, she decides to sell up and move away.

Mary Fortune

The Potted Gardener of the book title, Mary moves into Mrs Josephs' house after the murder in the previous book. She is a keen gardener who raises tropical plants in her conservatory and is also a superb baker, according to Mrs Bloxby. Agatha returns from a holiday to find Mary has become close to James. 'She's a remarkably good-looking lady and a great help at our horticultural society meetings,' Mrs Bloxby tells her.

'She and Mr Lacey are both such keen gardeners.' When Agatha first calls on her, 'the woman who answered the door made Agatha's heart sink. She was undoubtedly attractive, with a smooth, unlined face, blonde hair and bright-blue eyes.' Her house is decorated with green, which is also the only colour she wears.

Mary is murdered and left with her head stuck in the earth like a potted plant (hence, *Potted Gardener*). After the pair discover her body in the conservatory, Agatha is devastated when James reveals that he slept with Mary. Having assumed James led the life of a monk, she is crushed to find out he has 'lain in Mary's bed in Mary's arms. Her mind writhed under the weight of her miserable thoughts'.

Melissa Sheppard

In *Fairies of Fryfam*, while Agatha is away in Norfolk, this attractive divorcée moves to Carsely and is an instant hit with the Ladies' Society. Mrs Bloxby describes her as 'in her forties, blonde, very smart. Great sense of humour', causing an instant flash of jealousy in Agatha. Melissa pursues James and becomes his lover, but he is soon bored with her. On Agatha's return, James immediately proposes and Melissa is furious. However, James apparently sleeps with her again after the wedding.

In *Love from Hell*, Melissa becomes the next murder victim and James, who has disappeared, is suspected of the crime.

Deborah Fanshaw

Attractive divorcée who moves to the village in *Love, Lies and Liquor* and immediately begins to pursue 'Carsely's most wanted single man', James Lacey.

In her forties, rich and attractive and intent on marrying again, she is described as 'a tall, leggy woman with masses of brown curly hair and a great deal of energy'. Mrs Bloxby, however, finds her rather tiresome and, after Deborah vows to snare her man, she comments, 'I think she has too many hormones.'

Although James shows little interest in her, Deborah follows him to Snoth-on-Sea, where he is staying in a hotel with Agatha. James shows no interest and, after being washed out to sea by a freak wave, Deborah switches her affection to Charles as she recovers in hospital. Frightened by her over-zealous pursuit, Charles tells her that *he* is the one who is set to marry Agatha and, when Deborah goes to confront her love rival in the hotel room, she is shot through the head by a gunman.

Felicity Bross-Tilkington

Although she believes she is over James, Agatha is shocked to receive an invitation to his engagement in *Spoonful of Poison*. At the party, she is introduced to his bride-to-be and instantly feels

inadequate. 'Felicity was exquisite. She had wide-spaced grey eyes in a tanned face. Her thick brown hair cascaded down on her shoulders in an artful arrangement of waves and curls.' On the eve of the wedding in *There Goes the Bride*, James admits he doesn't want to go through with it, but it is too late to back out. When Felicity fails to turn up, and is found murdered at home, James and Agatha are both prime suspects.

In one of his more insightful moments, Charles tells Agatha that it will never work with James because he is a 'twenty-per-cent person'.

'You are an eighty-five-per-cent person and James only gives twenty per-cent. It's not a case of won't, it's a case of can't. A lot of men are like that but women will never understand. They go on giving. And they think if they go to bed with the twenty-per-center, and they give that last fifteen per cent, they'll miraculously wake up next to a hundred-per-center. Wrong. Anyway, if they wake up next to him it will be a miracle. Probably find a note on the pillow saying, 'Gone home to feed the dog,' or something like that.' (*Wizard of Evesham*)

Mrs Bloxby knows Agatha's obsessions of old. When Agatha begins to gush about the beauty of a Cotswold spring, she 'repressed a sigh'. 'Agatha was heading for another obsession, and while it lasted, the Cotswolds would be beautiful and every pop tune would have a special meaning.' (*Spoonful of Poison*)

10

The Raisin Detective Agency

A robbery which Agatha refers to as the 'Paris incident' prompts her to make her detecting legitimate, by setting up an agency. She hires an office in Mircester and advertises with the promise, 'All calls discreetly dealt with – video and electronic surveillance.'

Her first employees are her next-door neighbour, Mrs Emma Comfrey, and Carsely's unmarried mum, Miss Simms. She also employs a former press photographer and a surveillance expert on a freelance basis.

The bread and butter work consists of missing pets and evidence for divorce cases, and Agatha finds that tedious. But she gets her first major case in *Deadly Dance*, when an anxious mother employs her to protect her daughter, who has received a death threat in the run-up to her wedding.

Although business is booming, Agatha vows to retire from the firm and leave things in the charge of her colleagues after the wedding murder is solved in *There Goes the Bride*. But Agatha can never stay away for too long.

COMPANION

Emma Comfrey

Agatha's tall, thin, middle-aged neighbour, and a good detective until she develops an obsessive crush on Sir Charles Fraith. This leads to a hatred of Agatha and psychopathic behaviour.

Miss Simms

Carsely's unmarried mum is briefly employed by the agency until she meets Patrick Mulligan and decides to settle down.

Patrick Mulligan

A retired detective and 'a tall, cadaverous man who rarely smiles', he is hired by Agatha to clear up the backlog while she is embroiled in the case of the *Deadly Dance*, but he soon proves invaluable in solving bigger crimes. He is an ex-policeman with great contacts within the force, and can often find out information that Agatha is not privy to. After falling for Miss Simms, he asks her to marry him and she accepts. When they split, Patrick returns to the agency and once more becomes an asset to Agatha.

Mrs Freedman

Agatha's secretary from Evesham. 'Middle-aged, competent, quite a treasure.' She is always called by her second name, in the tradition of the Ladies' Society. She is plump, pleasant, with thick,

grey, curled hair, and never wears any make-up. Although efficient, she upsets Agatha by talking to the Boggles about a case in *Perfect Paragon*.

Phil Witherspoon

A Carsely villager and keen photographer who is looking to supplement his pension by working at the agency. At seventy-six, Agatha believes he is too old to be employed but, as a favour to her friend Mrs Bloxby, she employs him on a trial basis. He immediately helps Agatha find the body of a murdered teenager in *Perfect Paragon,* thereby earning the firm a huge amount of precious publicity. Agatha keeps him on and finds he often gains the trust of elderly women because of his age and courteous nature. A slim, average-sized man who still possesses thick grey hair, he has a face 'not so much lined as crumpled, as if one only had to take a hot iron to it to restore it to its former youth'.

Harry Beam

Mrs Freedman's nephew, who first appears in *Perfect Paragon* wearing a nose stud, dressed from head to toe in black and sporting a shaven head. Agatha believes he will be useless but gives him a day's trial. He impresses his potential boss by finding three cats and a dog in a few hours, and neglects to tell her that they were all at the animal shelter. He helps Agatha through his gap year before going to Oxford University and turns out to be a huge asset, particularly when cases involve hanging round in nightclubs. He also manages to win over potential suspects when he smartens up and turns out to be quite good-looking when dressed normally.

Toni Gilmour

A young girl from a rough council estate in Mircester who answers an ad for a trainee detective in *Kissing Christmas Goodbye*. Although she is not sure at first, Agatha is swayed by Toni's success in getting snaps of a cheating husband. She rescues her new employee from life with a violent brother and alcoholic mother and sets her up in a flat, giving her driving lessons and even buying an old car for her to drive.

Despite being sensible for a seventeen-year-old, Toni is almost raped on her first case when she agrees to meet a pub landlord at midnight, but Agatha follows her and comes to the rescue.

Pretty and blonde with 'pale-blue eyes fringed with thick, fair lashes in a neat-featured face', Toni is good at her new job and often gets to the answer before her boss. She brings out an almost maternal instinct in Agatha, who is torn between caring for her and jealousy at her youth and detecting success.

Toni's feelings about Agatha are equally mixed, soaring between gratitude for the difference she has made to her life, and the desire to be around younger people and to advance in the business without being tied to one agency. This dilemma is solved when, prompted by jealousy when Toni steals the limelight, Agatha suggests she helps the girl set up her own agency. However, Agatha's former employee, Harry Beam, steps in and offers to fund it himself, meaning the rival firm is now out of Agatha's control.

After a former classmate becomes their accountant and rips her company off, Toni returns to the fold, bringing best friend and colleague Sharon with her. However, she is still restless and fed up with being handed the minor cases. After confronting Agatha, who in a rare, honest moment admits she is jealous of her young colleague and promises to change, Toni feels, more than ever, that she can't leave.

Sharon Gold

Toni's best friend, who joins Agatha after the collapse of the second detective agency. Agatha finds her appearance off-putting. Sharon is a large girl who squeezes herself into inappropriately tight clothing and frequently changes the vibrant colour of her hair. But she is bright and sharp-witted, and is useful to Agatha because she fits in amongst the teens at trendy nightclubs and pubs, and therefore doesn't raise suspicion.

Paul Kenson and Fred Auster

After Toni and Sharon find a teenager who has gone missing in a highly publicized case, business is booming. Agatha decides to take on the two new sleuths, both in their forties and keen to leave the police force. Paul is 'thin, gangly and morose' and Fred is 'chubby and cheerful', but they are both excellent detectives.

11

Agatha's Cats

Never a feline fan before moving to the Cotswolds, Agatha is given her first pet by new friend Bill Wong. The gift of a tabby kitten comes after his mum's cat has a litter, and is intended to save it from a watery death. Agatha is initially dismayed by the odd present, and vows to get rid of it as soon as possible. However she soon falls for the cute creature, which she names Hodge, and worries that she has been 'reduced to the status of a village lady, drooling over an animal'.

On a trip to London, where she has temporarily rented a flat, she loses Hodge and, after searching high and wide, tracks him down in Cornwall Square. On her return to the flat, she finds the real Hodge lying contentedly on the kitchen chair and realizes the other tabby is a stray. As the pair seem to get on, Agatha decides to keep him and takes him back to Carsely. Having learned that Hodge was the name of Samuel Johnson's cat, she keeps up the literary reference by calling the newcomer Boswell, after Johnson's biographer.

Although she is not a natural pet lover, Agatha's cats Hodge and Boswell are the one permanence in her life and she cares deeply for them. She sees no irony in the fact that she cooks them fresh fish and chicken livers for dinner, while happily dining on microwaved curries herself. She often plays with them and pampers them, and their instinctive reaction to danger has saved her from certain death on many occasions.

In *Witch of Wyckhadden*, Agatha adopts a third cat after finding it wandering on the promenade, starving and dirty. She believes it to be the creature which attacked her when she found Francie Juddle's body, and takes it back to her hotel, where she feeds it up and calls it Scrabble. When she returns to Carsely, however, she feels it is unfair to her other two cats to keep it, so her kindly cleaner, Doris Simpson, takes Scrabble in.

12
Itchy Feet

Although she spends the greater part of her time there, Agatha's adventures are by no means confined to the Cotswolds. Murder and mayhem occur wherever she travels, whether it is in the UK or abroad. She enjoys foreign travel, although she insists on five-star treatment wherever she goes, and she has occasionally taken breaks – willingly or otherwise – in English resorts.

Wyckhadden

Agatha hides in the old-fashioned seaside town while her hair, destroyed by a vengeful hairdresser, grows back. 'There is nothing more depressing for a middle-aged, lovelorn woman with bald patches on her head than to find herself in an English seaside resort out of season.' A windy promenade displays torn posters and old summer bunting and a cobbled side street boasts holiday homes painted in pastel colours. The prosperity of the town in the late nineteenth and early twentieth centuries has disappeared as cheap foreign holidays entice people abroad.

Agatha stays in a faded Victorian boarding house called the Garden Hotel and drinks in a dingy pub, The Dog and Duck.

Fryfam

After a wrecked engagement to Jimmy Jessop, and still pining for lost love James, Agatha seeks solace in this tiny fictional Norfolk village, where she has rented a house called Lavender Cottage. Fryfam has a large village green surrounded by flint cottages, a pub called the Green Dragon and a church, and is something of a step back in time when it comes to values. The locals are a tight-knit, superstitious and often unfriendly bunch.

Snoth-on-Sea

Fictional Sussex seaside town where James enjoyed idyllic holidays as a child. After returning to his cottage in *Love, Lies and Liquor*, he takes Agatha on a mystery break, only to find that the town has become dirty and shabby and the Palace Hotel, the

grand guest house of his youth, is now a grim B&B. To top it all, the pair are caught up in a murder when Agatha's scarf is used to strangle another guest.

Hewes and Downboys

Hewes is an attractive market town in Sussex, built along a river, where Agatha and her friends go to attend James and Felicity's wedding in *There Goes the Bride*. It also boasts a picturesque marina and a pleasant pub-cum-hotel where the party stay.

In the neighbouring village of Downboys, the bride's family owns a huge estate which backs on to the water. The village is built around a crossroads and has a pub, a church and a grocery store. 'It seemed a very gloomy sort of place.'

Kyrenia

Following their ruined wedding day, James flees to Kyrenia, in Northern Cyprus, where they were due to have spent their honeymoon. Agatha, of course, flies out in pursuit and books into the resort's real Dome Hotel.

'The Dome Hotel is a large building on the waterfront at Kyrenia, Turkish name Girne, which has seen better days and has a certain battered colonial grandeur. There is something endearing about the Dome.' Agatha's room has a balcony overlooking the Mediterranean and a seawater pool carved out of rock.

Later she moves to the villa that James is borrowing from a friend for an extended stay, which is near the Onar Village Hotel.

While there, she visits Famagusta (Gazimagusa), the second largest city in Northern Cyprus and described as 'one of the most remarkable ruins in the world'. Shakespeare's *Othello* was possibly set here and Agatha visits the local landmark known as Othello's Tower, a Lusignan citadel built to protect the harbour and reconstructed by the Venetians in 1492.

After meeting a group of holiday-makers, she dines with them at a restaurant called the Grapevine, which is a favourite with British tourists. Later they eat at the Ottoman House restaurant in Zeytinlik and also at the fish restaurant, the Altinkaya, which backs on to their villa. All three are actual eateries in the area.

Together they also travel to Nicosia (Leftkosa to the Turkish population) and visit the covered market. 'The centre of Nicosia was a pleasant, friendly place with a lot of interesting old buildings and shops.'

Robinson Crusoe Island

After James flees to a monastery in France, Agatha decides to get away from it all and to lick her wounds in *Day the Floods Came*. She chooses the remote South American island where Alexander

Selkirk was stranded for four years from 1704, inspiring the Daniel Defoe classic, *Robinson Crusoe*. The island, just off the coast of Chile, is in the Juan Fernandez Archipelago and reachable by a small plane from Tobalaba Airport in Santiago. This terrifying flight, and the bumpy Jeep ride to the resort, is not Agatha's cup of tea, but the hotel, the Panglas, turns out to be stunning, and she meets a friendly group of fellow travellers. However, the tropical paradise she imagined turns out to be a rocky, barren land and she learns that Defoe set his own tale in the Caribbean instead of Selkirk's true location.

Istanbul

A favourite city of author M.C. Beaton. Agatha travels there, in *There Goes the Bride*, on her way to visit the site of the Charge of the Light Brigade in the Crimea. She is hoping to impress the recently engaged James, who accused her of never listening to him, with her knowledge of military history.

She has previously stayed in the Pera Palace Hotel, made famous by Agatha Christie's *Murder on the Orient Express*, but this time she opts for a hotel on the other side of the Golden Horn in the Sultan Ahmet district 'under the shadow of the Blue Mosque'. The real Artifes, in the heart of the Old City, boasts a rooftop restaurant and views over the Marmara Sea.

On her return she visits the tourist sites, including

the splendid domed sixth-century basilica, the Ayasofya, which is now a museum, and the Spice Market, where James Bond was blown up in *From Russia with Love*. On finding out her James is off to Gallipoli, the site of the disastrous Allied landings in the First World War, Agatha changes her plans. Unfortunately, James spots her there and thinks he is being stalked.

The Crimea

From Istanbul, Agatha catches a 'Russian rust bucket' to Balaclava in the Crimea, the only autonomous state in the Ukraine. The boat is full of Ukrainian women and manned by a Russian crew who speak no English, and the only food she can face is soup. Two days of sailing across the Black Sea take her to the Dakkar Resort hotel which offers 'the blessings of a civilized hotel with a smiling, beautiful receptionist and a well-appointed room'. Instead of showing her the site of the Charge of the Light Brigade, the famous Crimean War battle, her guide drags her round one Soviet Second World War memorial after another. Finally Agatha gets to the battlefield, but she is sadly disappointed as it is now merely a plain full of vineyards. When James and his fiancée arrive, Agatha flees the hotel and catches a plane back to Istanbul.

Paris

Agatha pops over to Paris in many a book, including *There Goes the Bride* when she is foolishly pursuing Frenchman Sylvan

Dubois. After calling him, and finding he has a woman in bed with him, she leaves the city in shame.

In *Deadly Dance*, Agatha is prompted to open her own detective agency after her purse is stolen on the Metro and the police treat her with disdain. On this occasion, in a rare fit of thrift, she has booked into a small hotel off St-Germain-des-Prés in the Latin Quarter, but soon regrets the decision as the heat rises to 105°F and her room has no air-conditioning.

Later, she and Charles fly to Paris to interview Felicity Felliat, the daughter of a friend of Charles who was supposed to be working for a couturier in the Rue St-Honoré. They stay in the Hôtel Duval on the Boulevard St-Michel, where suspect Jeremy Laggatt-Brown claimed to have been staying when his daughter was shot at. They walk by the Seine and eat at Maubert-Mutiliaté. While she is there, a hitman is found dead in her kitchen at home.

Later they return and find a drunk by the fountain on Place Maubert, who helps them solve the case.

13
Mrs Raisin's Reason

A fertile mind, a belligerent soul and a propensity to argue mean there is never a dull moment when Agatha is around. Not one to take the accepted view as read, she has her own brand of logic which can throw up pearls of wisdom, or purely perverse argument. The following are random thoughts from the mind of the great detective:

> 'Not for the first time, Agatha wondered about British Rail's use of the word "terminate". One just expected the train to blow apart. Why not just say "stops here"?' *Quiche of Death.*

> When Roy remarks, 'Age does bring wisdom,' Agatha replies: 'Not really. I've found that stupid young people grow up to be stupid old people.' *Perfect Paragon.*

'How strange that few people talked about love any more. They were obsessed, taken hostage or co-dependent – anything rather than admit they were not in control, for the word "love" now meant weakness.' *Terrible Tourist.*

'People always talked about hearts breaking but the pain was always right in the gut.' *Wellspring of Death.*

Reasoning that the countryside is more damaging to the environment than her smoking: 'I just read that a farting cow produces more damage to the ozone layer than a four-wheel drive.' *Spoonful of Poison.*

After spotting neighbour Paul Chatterton eyeing up a young secretary in a short skirt:

'It just wasn't fair on middle-aged women. If she eyed up a young man, she would be considered a harpy. But a man of the same age, provided he had kept his figure, would never be regarded with the same contempt.' *Haunted House.*

Agatha's Niggles

Many everyday irritations make Agatha's hackles rise, from the opening hours of British shops to the smoking ban. Here are a few of her bugbears:

After her train grinds to a halt for no apparent reason, and the passengers sit stoically waiting: 'Why are we like sheep that have gone astray?' wondered Agatha. 'Why are the British so cowed and placid? Why does no one shout for the guard and demand to know the reason? Other, more voluble, races would not stand for it.' *Quiche of Death.*

The lady whose voice is on Call Minder always seemed to Agatha to be an irritating relic of the

days when women took elocution lessons. It was a governessy, eat-your-porridge-or-you-won't-go-to-the-circus sort of voice. "Two messages," said the voice. "Would you like to hear them?" Did anyone *not* want to hear messages? thought Agatha crossly. *Wellspring of Death.*

Agatha is annoyed to find a garage closed on Saturday. 'Isn't that so bloody British? No wonder half our businesses are being outsourced abroad.' *There Goes the Bride.*

A frequent beef of Agatha's is the closing of local police stations in rural areas. She believes the police in towns such as Mircester are overstretched. 'Crime has spread in the countryside in a big way,' she grumbles. 'Do you know, the farmers can't even leave their combine harvesters out in the field at night? One farmer found that they had pinched the whole thing, dismantled it and shipped it off.' *Deadly Dance.*

14
Raisin's Questions

How well do you know the redoubtable Mrs Raisin? Test your knowledge with a fun quiz and see if you are a super-sleuth or a rank amateur.

- What is the name of the cat that Agatha rescued from Wyckhadden and gave to Doris Simpson?

- The cottage next door to Agatha was known by which exotic and inappropriate name before James bought it?

- Shortly before James's wedding to Felicity in *There Goes the Bride*, Agatha travelled to the Ukraine to visit the site of which famous battle?

- How did James get out of the country when he fled Carsely, and Agatha, suffering from a brain tumour?

- What is the name of Charles's distinctly unfriendly manservant?

- Which large PR firm did Agatha sell out to?

- Which famous artist's painting was stolen from the manor in *Fairies of Fryfam*?

- What caused Deborah Fanshawe to be hailed a heroine in *Love, Lies and Liquor*?

- Charles lives with his elderly aunt. What is her name?

- What was the occupation of Agatha's neighbour, John Armitage?

- Who ran the dried flower shop in Carsely before becoming involved in a murder plot in *Vicious Vet*?

- What was unusual about the serving staff at the party on the eve of James's wedding to Felicity?

- Which garden gift did Agatha proudly present to Doris Simpson on her return from a stay in London, only to have it given back a little later?

- Who funded Toni's ill-fated venture into her own private detective business?

- What was the name of the awful old couple who Agatha was trapped into taking out for a day in Bath?

- Where were Agatha and James due to go on their honeymoon after the ill-fated wedding day ruined by Jimmy's arrival?

Agatha Raisin
COMPANION

- What does elderly villager Mr Crinsted teach Agatha in *Curious Curate*?

- What is Doris Simpson's husband called?

- What does Agatha get the up-and-coming pop group Stepping Out to promote in *Love from Hell*?

- What is the name of Paul Chatterton's fiery Spanish wife?

ANSWERS

- Scrabble

- New Delhi

- The Charge of the Light Brigade

- He hitched a ride to France on a friend's boat

- Gustav

- Pedmans

- Stubbs

- She was swept out to sea by a wave and miraculously survived

- Mrs Tassy

- He was a crime writer

- Josephine Webster

- They were naked

- A gnome

- Harry Beam

- The Boggles

- Northern Cyprus

- Chess

- Bert

- Walking boots

- Juanita

15
Raisin's Recipes

Although she is keen to try the local food when abroad, there's nothing Agatha likes more than good solid English cooking. Happier with ham, egg and chips or a fried breakfast than a Caesar salad, she loves stodge and often pays for it with her waistline.

STODGY STEAK AND KIDNEY PUDDING

A pub favourite, this hearty English dish is just the sort of good comfort food Agatha loves to tuck into.

INGREDIENTS

675g/1½lb chuck steak, cubed
225g/8oz ox kidney, cut into
   2.5 cm/1 inch cubes
1 medium onion, peeled and
   finely chopped
Pinch of salt
2 tbsp plain flour
2 bay leaves
150 ml/¼ pint beef stock

FOR THE PASTRY

400g/14oz self-raising flour
200g/7oz beef or vegetarian
   suet
290ml/½ pint
   cold water

To make the pastry, sift the flour into a large mixing bowl and add a pinch of salt. Mix in the suet using a knife. Then add a few drops of water and continue to blend. Keep adding water until you have a sticky dough.

Knead the dough with your hands and form a ball.

Roll the dough on a lightly floured surface until it is approx 1cm (½ inch) thick.

Cut off a quarter of the dough and use the rest to line a 3-pint (175ml) pudding basin, with a decent overhang.

Now mix the meat, onion, bay leaves, salt and flour together and place in the bottom of the basin.

Add the beef stock.

Roll the remaining dough out to form the pastry lid, place on top and then fold the overhang on to it, pressing together to seal.

Grease a double length of foil to go over the top, creased in the middle to allow it to expand. Tie this on with string.

Place an old plate, upturned, in a saucepan of water and put the pudding on top.

Steam for five hours, making sure you don't let the saucepan run dry.

ICKY STICKY PUDDING

This pudding originated in the Lake District but is a popular choice in many restaurants in the Cotswolds and is a particular favourite of Agatha's.

INGREDIENTS

340g/12oz dates
2 tsp bicarbonate of soda
125g/4oz diced butter
340g/12oz brown sugar
4 eggs
400g/14oz self-raising flour
1 tsp vanilla essence
500ml water

FOR THE SAUCE

340g/12oz soft brown sugar
250ml/8fl oz whipping cream
250g/8oz unsalted butter
2 tsp vanilla essence

Chop the dates and put into a saucepan with the bicarbonate of soda and water.

Boil for five minutes and allow to cool until it is just warm.

Add the butter and sugar and stir well until dissolved and melted.

Lightly beat the eggs and add to the warm pan, then mix in the flour and vanilla essence.

Pour into a greased 24 cm/9-inch cake tin and bake in a moderate oven at 160°C (320°F, gas mark 3) for an hour.

When the pudding is ready to serve, make the toffee sauce by putting all the ingredients in a pan over a low heat until the sugar has dissolved and the sauce has thickened and darkened in colour.

Spoon over the pudding to serve.

MRS BLOXBY'S TERRIFIC TEACAKES

INGREDIENTS
450g/1lb plain flour
1 tsp salt
2 tsp sugar

100g/4oz currants or mixed dried fruits
25g/1oz yeast
300ml/½ pint milk

Sift the flour into a mixing bowl and add salt, sugar and currants.

Warm the milk and use a little to cream the yeast.

Make a well in the centre of the flour and pour milk and yeast mixture in, then scatter some of the flour over the top and leave in a warm place for ten minutes.

Add the remaining milk and knead into a dough.

Cover with clingfilm or a cloth and leave in a warm place for at least an hour to rise.

Divide into eight balls and flatten to make teacake shapes.

Place on a greased baking sheet, prick with a fork and leave for a further 30 minutes.

Brush with egg or melted butter and bake in a pre-heated oven at 220°C (425°F, gas mark 7).

Serve warm with butter.

SPINACH QUICHE TO DIE FOR
(No cowbane included)

This recipe uses frozen spinach, so it cannot be easily mistaken for deadly plants.

INGREDIENTS

300g/10oz frozen chopped
spinach, thawed and drained
250g/8oz Cheddar cheese, grated
175g/6oz Feta cheese
1 medium onion, chopped
100g/3oz butter
3 sprigs fresh thyme

4 eggs, beaten
250ml/½ pint milk

FOR THE PASTRY

175g/6oz plain flour
75g/2¾ oz butter
290ml/½ pint cold water

(If you want to cheat, as Agatha almost certainly would, buy ready-made shortcrust pastry instead.)

Make the pastry by sifting the flour into a large bowl, then rub in the butter until you have a crumbly mixture. Slowly add enough cold water so that you have a firm dough, then place in the fridge for half an hour.

Roll the dough out on a lightly floured surface and line a 22cm/8-inch greased flan dish leaving the extra pastry hanging over the side.

Chill in the fridge.

Melt the butter in a saucepan and sauté the onion until lightly browned. Stir in the spinach, thyme, Feta cheese and half the Cheddar cheese.

Spoon into the chilled pastry case.

Whisk together the eggs and milk and pour over the spinach mixture in the pastry case.

Bake at 190°C (375°F, gas mark 5) for 15 minutes.

Remove from the oven and sprinkle the remaining cheese on top and bake for another 35–40 minutes.

Allow to stand before serving hot or cold.

Index